What people are saying about ...

THE FAR BANK

"I count Zeke Pipher as one of my heroes. I've been covering the outdoor world for over thirty years and Zeke is on my short list of 'must read' colleagues. His devotional, *In Pursuit: Devotions for the Hunter and Fisherman*, is one I've read cover to cover multiple times, and I always look forward to his thoughtful and well-written magazine articles. In short, I read anything and everything Zeke produces, especially when he has the chance to weave spiritual insight into his outdoor adventures as he does in *The Far Bank*. I can think of no one more qualified and capable of penning a devotional for anglers."

Scott Bestul, *Field & Stream* magazine field editor and columnist

"I admire Zeke's ability to balance his passion for the outdoors with his faith and family, and his writing resonates with many. *The Far Bank* is another insightful and inspiring work."

Vicki Cianciarulo, cohost of *Archer's Choice* and *The Choice* television shows

"Though I have yet to fish with Zeke, I have been with him many times in his primary endeavor as a follower of Christ and a fisher of men. Zeke is a committed man of God who understands the importance of spending time in nature's solitude and how a day outside with the Lord is good for the soul."

Dr. Tom Osborne, former University of Nebraska football coach and athletic director, former US Representative

"Zeke does an excellent job keeping the reader intrigued through fishing stories while applying biblical applications for everyday life. *The Far Bank* is an excellent book for Christian anglers, one that's hard to put down."

Pam Martin-Wells, bass fishing coach at Emmanuel University, Bassmaster pro angler, six-time Ladies Bass Anglers Association (LBAA) Angler of the Year

"From the very first page, this remarkable collection of biblical devotionals captured my heart and mind in a way that only a true passion can. Fishing, a lifelong love of mine, serves as a brilliant backdrop for understanding God's profound messages of love and purpose. Each devotional skillfully intertwines fishing examples with biblical principles, making the lessons not only relatable but deeply impactful. This book invites readers into a relationship with God that transcends mere rules; it emphasizes the beauty of connection over a checklist of do's and don'ts. Prepare to be hooked—just like I was—eager to dive deeper into the next insight and examine your heart in response to God's enduring love and truth."

Alton Jones, Sr., Bassmaster pro angler

"*The Far Bank* made me reflect on my experiences that have led me to where I am now. I used to fly fish with an enthusiastic desire to catch every fish in the river. I netted thousands of trout. Some were giants. A few were state records. One was close to a world record. Yet, success on the water didn't satisfy my heart. The gospel alone has done that for me. Today, I enter the river to enjoy God's goodness and soak up as much of His truth and beauty as possible. Joy in fishing is about something other than our performance. It's about God's grace toward us, and Zeke celebrates that truth well in this book. Zeke takes readers into the water, into adventure, so that we can know and enjoy our Lord. From one trout bum to another, I strongly recommend this book."

Jason Hamrick, fly fishing instructor, fishing guide, and owner of Cowboy Drifters (Casper, WY)

"I happen to love two things Zeke loves: fly fishing and the gospel. You don't have to love either to enjoy this book, but you may end up treasuring both. With heart and art, Zeke invites us to connect with the beauty of God's creation, the possibilities of His grace, and the gift of new life. These 40 devotional reflections are a well-timed mercy to my own heart, as they will be to many."

Scotty Smith, pastor emeritus, Christ Community Church (Franklin, TN); teacher in residence, West End Community Church (Nashville, TN)

ZEKE PIPHER

THE FAR BANK

40 DEVOTIONS FOR ANGLERS

150 YEARS STRONG
DAVID C COOK

THE FAR BANK
Published by David C Cook
4050 Lee Vance Drive
Colorado Springs, CO 80918 U.S.A.

Integrity Music Limited, a Division of David C Cook
Brighton, East Sussex BN1 2RE, England

Details in some stories have been changed to protect the identities of the persons involved.

The author has added italics to Scripture quotations for emphasis.

Library of Congress Control Number 2024952346
ISBN 978-0-8307-8787-6
eISBN 978-0-8307-8788-3

The Team: Luke McKinnon, Jeff Gerke, Gina Pottenger, Karissa Silvers, Susan Murdock
Cover Design: James Hershberger

Printed in the United States of America
First Edition 2025

1 2 3 4 5 6 7 8 9 10

050625

To Heartland EFC, the strong and stable boat that has loved our family well.

CONTENTS

FOREWORD

I am a biased reader. I am a follower of Jesus. I am a fool who fly fishes. This foreword is far more than a testimony of praise for *The Far Bank*. It is a humble attempt to invite you into a world of mystery that is seldom waded into by those who love God.

While Zeke wrote *The Far Bank* for all kinds of anglers, those souls who fly fish know at a deep, resonant level that one can do everything well—pick the right fly, cast to the perfect spot with a gravity-free drift—and come up with nothing.

Nothing?

No, not nothing, far better than nothing: the loss of hope that is rectified by the courage to change flies and cast again.

One can lose and regain hope a thousand times and still walk away from the day empty-handed. It is a mystery. It is a raw, uncontrollable, passionately profound mystery that our perfection, or illusion thereof, may not bring what our hearts most deeply desire to our hands.

This humble grasp of reality makes my time with fly-fishing friends more alive with God than what I often experience with my more pedantic, non-fly-fishing church friends. These church friends think fly fishing is a hobby. It is pointless to disabuse them. Fly fishing is no more a hobby than any other spiritual discipline.

I don't fly fish to catch trout. I fish for trout to catch me. Each tug on the line pulls me into a realm I can see but can't truly see. It is like looking into the reflection of a mirror where we see only in part, but I know one day I will see face-to-face, and I shall know fully, even as I am fully known. For many, this will sound either baroque or like a self-justification to buy another rod and call it godly.

Let me further clarify: I don't fly fish with people who are competitive and need to catch fish. I find these zealots tedious and shallow. I fish with those who know that every fish is a gift, undeserved, no matter how good you are at your craft. I fish with men and women who are humbled by the glory of what is around them and delighted by every fish their friends catch. I can fish alone, but the reality of our existence is that where two or more are gathered, there is our Creator.

Fly fishing saved my life. It is too long a story, but I kiss every fish I catch to thank them for yanking me out of the realm of mastery, competence, competition, and control that was killing my soul and body. Fly fishing took me into an experience of beauty that, other than my wife, has given me my best glimpse of the face of God.

I love this wise, playful, honest, and compelling devotional. If you change the words "fly fishing" to "reading Scripture" in all the preceding paragraphs, you'll know why I am writing this in support of *The Far Bank*. Reading Scripture has saved my life. It gives me a glimpse of mystery and beauty that takes my breath away and humbles me with the undeserved gifts I occasionally catch after many casts and changes of flies.

We often approach Scripture as we do any other endeavor: know the right stuff, do the right thing, do it long enough, and you'll get what you have worked to attain. It is a lie. The Bible is 70 percent story, and stories are deep runs with much meaning, but they require humble and persistent engagement to fathom. You don't drop a line, catch a fish, and get what you came for. Instead, you sit, watch, and feel the rhythm of the water and wait for the movement of the text to bring you the heartache of truth and the compelling glory of grace. It is a gift, not a task.

This brilliant devotional is written by a lover of grace, beauty, moving water, and the reflection of the face of God in the wonder of what is learned when we peer below the surface. Let it catch you. Sit and wait. Let your heart be stirred, and open your eyes to what is there but can't be seen despite your best efforts.

Let the tug of the line raise your dopamine and cortisol. But be aware that every tug is but a pull into what your heart most deeply desires, and that is to be face-to-face with the Creator of the wild colors of brown trout. If you let your heart receive the gift of grace, your life, let alone your fishing, will be filled with wonder and gratitude. Tight lines.

Dan B. Allender, PhD
Professor of Counseling Psychology, Founding President
The Seattle School of Theology and Psychology

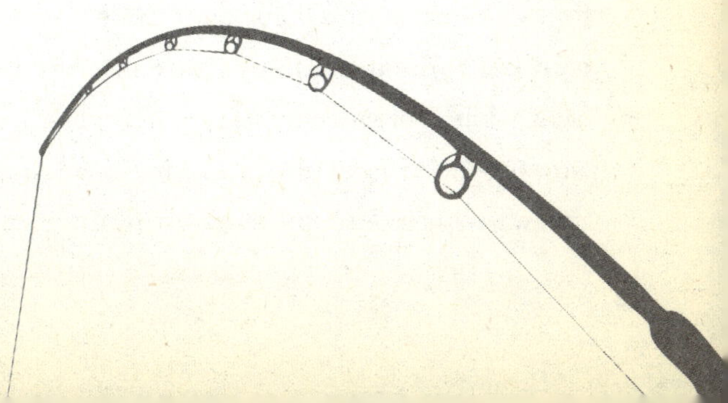

INTRODUCTION

I wrote many of these devotions while sitting in a folding chair beside the Miracle Mile in Wyoming, the Eleven Mile Canyon in Colorado, and the "Holy Waters" of the Au Sable River in Michigan. I crafted some at our kitchen table after throwing top-water lures with friends on Mariposa Lake. I wrote this introduction on an airplane the day after fishing Lake Huron with the friends I describe in chapter 25. As I typed these words into my laptop, the tips of my fingers still smelled like the oily skin of the steelhead I'd landed the previous day.

I wrote these devotions by my favorite waters, hoping you could read them as you fish your favorite lakes, rivers, streams, or oceans. I realize that's unlikely, if for no other reason than there are forty chapters in *The Far Bank*, and who among us gets forty days a year to fish?

For this reason, I packed this book with stories. When we can't fish, we can at least tell our tales. Simply recounting a great moment outdoors enlivens the heart. I live in central Nebraska, eight hours from a blue-ribbon trout stream. Yet when I call up the memory of entering the Missouri River in Montana last April and how the icy-cold waters suctioned my waders to my calves, it gives me goose bumps.

My hope is that these upcoming stories will captivate you the way seeing a river delighted the Mole in *The Wind in the Willows*:

> He thought his happiness was complete when, as he meandered aimlessly along, suddenly he stood by the edge of a full-fed river. Never in his life had he seen a river before—this sleek, sinuous, full-bodied animal, chasing and chuckling, gripping things with a gurgle and leaving them with a laugh, to fling itself on fresh playmates that shook themselves free, and were caught and held again. All was a-shake and a-shiver—glints and gleams and sparkles, rustle and swirl, chatter and bubble. The Mole was bewitched, entranced, fascinated.[1]

My more profound hope, however, is that these devotions help you find renewal and strength in our God who loves you with the infinitely vast heart of a Father. Our vibrancy and joy aren't sourced in water or fishing but in knowing the One who created the seas and caused them to "swarm with swarms of living creatures" (Gen. 1:20a).

My prayer for you is: "Jesus, as You created the heavens and earth to be good and teem with life, may You also bring goodness and fullness of life to my fellow angler reading this book."

If you join me in this journey, I will commit to steering us away from two popular errors of our day. First, we will avoid the hazards of rationalism and modernism. These worldviews seek to remove the wonder and mystery of God to make Him easier to comprehend. Easier to predict. Easier to control. Yet that is not our God. As the third devotion celebrates, our God is infinite, and we are finite. This means, quite literally, that though we will have all eternity to learn about Him, we will always have an infinite amount to discover. May we remain amazed at His glory and greatness.

Second, we will avoid the dangers of an experience-driven, feelings-based interpretation of the Bible. This is often called the reader-response approach to Scripture. It suggests that how the reader thinks and feels about a passage should play a prominent role in the meaning of the text. This is a treacherous way to approach theology, leading us away from what the author, inspired by the Spirit of God, has communicated. *When rightly understood*, there is power in the Word of God, and we will do our best to handle each passage with humility and integrity.

Let's be honest: anglers are known to exaggerate. I did my best not to add an inch to any fish in the stories ahead. However, I changed some of the names and situational details to protect the anonymity of the people involved and, if I'm being honest, the precise locations of my favorite fishing spots.

The fishing-related quotes at the start of each devotion are from some of my favorite books. That may seem like an odd thing to mention, but it's important to me that you know that I didn't just grab them from the internet when I wrote the book. These statements grabbed me over the years, and I can recommend each book referenced in the upcoming pages.

Why forty devotions? When I consider the forty years that Israel wandered in the wilderness and the forty days that Jesus faced Satan's temptations, it seems that God purposely chose forty as a unit of time for testing people to see if they would consider His words and trust them. May we be challenged during these forty days, and may we prove faithful to "every word that comes from the mouth of God" (Matt. 4:4b).

Where we're going, the waters are deep. I can't even promise they're safe. But they're pure and powerful and will change your life if you let them.

Zeke Pipher
June 2024
Central City, Nebraska

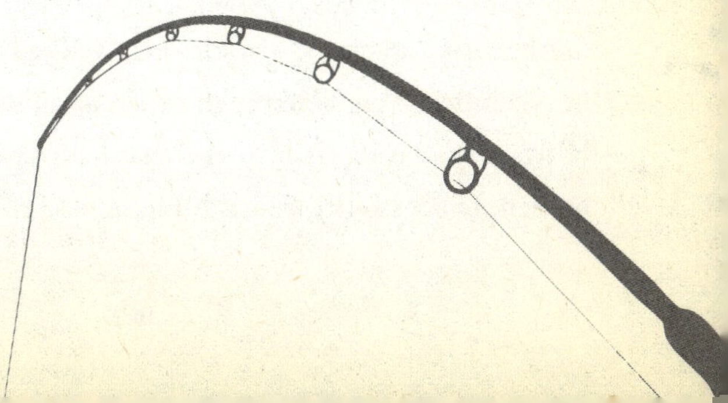

1

THE FAR BANK

But as for me, I am tormented with an everlasting itch for things remote. I love to sail forbidden seas, and land on barbarous coasts.

Herman Melville, *Moby-Dick*

Scripture to Read: Psalm 16

The public pull-off area along the Madison River looked like a parking lot at Disney World in the summer. When I first arrived in Ennis, Montana, I visited one of the town's many fly shops. The man behind the counter directed me to a stretch of the river south of town. It must have been the same place he'd directed all his customers; dozens of anglers lined the bank just beyond the horde of vehicles. For two days, I joined the masses and fished that spot. I caught a few small rainbows and several mountain whitefish, but nothing like the fish the Madison is famous for.

At the end of the second day, as I slipped my rod into the carrier on the top of my truck, an older man walked up to the vehicle parked beside mine. We greeted each other, and he asked if I could spare a bottle of water. I gave him one that had started the day frozen, had melted, but was still ice-cold. He held it to his forehead, then the back of his neck, and then he opened it and drank it without stopping to breathe.

I offered him another, and the two of us leaned on our trucks and talked about fishing while a brilliant sunset emerged on the big sky canvas. As often happens after a day outdoors, two unfamiliar but grateful anglers became friends in a parking lot near the water. Within twenty minutes, Ralph and I were showing each other photos of our families and exchanging flies from our fly boxes.

Before we parted ways, Ralph said, "If you cross this channel by that stump over there, it stays shallow enough that you can get to that middle island."

He pointed toward what I'd been assuming was the other side of the river. It wasn't, Ralph explained. A long, thin enclave separated the touristy half of the river from the part the locals fished.

"Walk across that island, wade to the middle of the next channel, then cast to the far bank." He winked. "That's where the big ones are."

The following day, I broke away from the pack of anglers by the Disney World parking area. I walked downriver to the stump, entered the river, and leaned into the current, shuffling my wader boots along the slippery rocks toward the island. It took half an hour to reach the far bank. The current was noticeably stronger than where I'd been fishing the first two days. The water was deeper and thus more mysterious and quite a bit colder than the shallows I had waded the day before.

I didn't see another person for six hours, just the dark black spots on thick-bellied rainbows as they swam out of my net and back into the depths below.

The journey to know and enjoy God calls us to a place that others often avoid—the realm of the heart, its affections and motivations. It requires a teachable spirit, one eager for counsel from those who have traveled further.

The journey also involves bookwork. God reveals Himself to us through His Holy Scriptures, and we pursue Him primarily through studying His Word. For slow readers (this author included), this can feel like hard work, like shuffling wader boots on slippery rocks against a forceful current.

But reading the Bible is the easy part. The exacting task is allowing the Scriptures to confront our sins and correct the lies we believe. Through the Holy Scriptures, the Spirit shows us the good, true, and beautiful things of God and what He has made. As God reveals His truth to us, He shows us where we fall short. How we're hurting others, perhaps. How we're being selfish. How we love created things more than our Creator. If we have eyes to see, the Scriptures will show us what needs to be confessed, corrected, and changed in our lives.

> The word of God is living and active, sharper than any two-edged sword, piercing to the division of soul and of spirit, of joints and of marrow, and discerning the thoughts and intentions of the heart. And no creature is hidden from his sight, but all are naked and exposed to the eyes of him to whom we must give account. (Heb. 4:12–13)

One might ask, "Why would we do this difficult work?"

The answer is: For the sake of joy. For the sake of our flourishing and spiritual well-being. Even if it's painful to hear, God tells us the truth in order to set us free to live a full, vibrant life with Him. Jesus says in John 8:31b–32: "If you abide in my word, you are truly my disciples, and you will know the truth, and the truth will set you free."

As hard as it is to read and believe the Bible, confess our sins, and receive the grace and mercy of God through faith in Jesus, it is the only path of life. King David shows us this in Psalm 16, when he writes, "I say to the LORD, 'You are my Lord; I have no good apart from you'" (v. 2). He's declaring that God is what he wants most. At this point in his life, he is fervently pursuing the Lord. He's praying. He's listening. He's meditating on the Scriptures. Day and night, he seeks God's counsel. He guards his heart from other gods because he knows that treasuring anything more than the Lord multiplies sorrows (v. 4).

Psalm 16:11 is one of my favorite verses in the Bible, for it shows us what we find when we pursue God through His Word: "You make known to me the path of life; in your presence there is fullness of joy; at your right hand are pleasures forevermore."

The path of life. Fullness of joy. Pleasures forevermore. These aren't merely poetic phrases, though they do read beautifully. These are David's objective findings and actual experiences. And they can be true for us today if we go with David to the far bank. The Lord guides us, and He guarantees our success, as Proverbs 8:17 promises, "I love those who love me, and those who seek me diligently find me."

QUESTIONS FOR FURTHER REFLECTION:

1. How much is the Word of God shaping your thoughts, feelings, and opinions compared to all the other intakes in your life, such as social media, television, movies, sports, and friends?

2. Jesus asks in Luke 6:46, "Why do you call me, 'Lord, Lord,' and do not do what I say?" (NIV). Is your time in the Scriptures changing your life, leading you toward becoming more like Jesus? Are there ways that you are calling Jesus "Lord" but not obeying the life-giving commands He gives?
3. Can you describe a time when reading, believing, and applying a truth in the Bible thrilled your heart and gave direction to your situation?

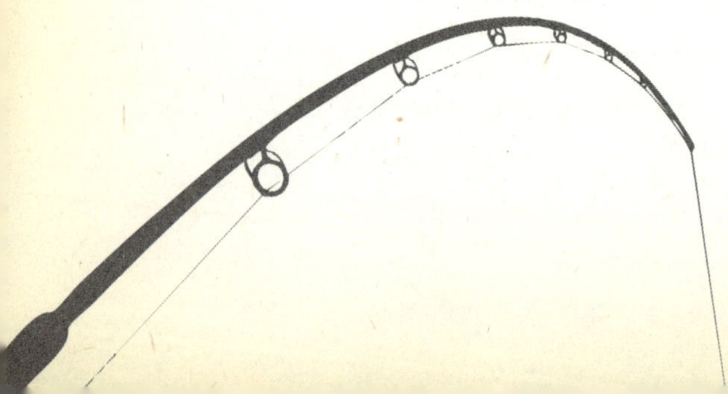

2

WILDLY GENEROUS

When they go fishing, it is not really fish they are after. It is a philosophic meditation.

E. T. Brown, *Not Without Prejudice: Essays on Assorted Subjects*

Scripture to Read: John 14:1–17; 16:7–11

"I'll show you what little I know," Scott said.

"Little" proved to be a gross understatement.

I met Scott years ago on a Sunday morning in the foyer of our church. When he mentioned his love for fly fishing, I told him I'd always wanted to learn. That's when he made the offer, inviting me to his acreage the following afternoon.

When I arrived, Scott was threading a fly line and leader through the eyelets of a rod. He tied on a giant black leech, then snipped off the hook with wire cutters.

"We don't need to snag grass today," he said.

With the patience and practicality of all good teachers, Scott walked me through the entire fly-fishing process. He taught me how to tie the Eugene bend, nail, and triple surgeon knots. He showed me how to cast, retrieve, and mend lines. He explained the numbering system for fly lines, leaders, and tippets. He also gave me a brief overview of entomology while showing me his flies, many of which he'd tied.

As we were wrapping up, he asked me, "When do you think you'll go?"

When I told him I hoped to go to Colorado in a few weeks, he pulled out a map of the South Platte. He grabbed a pencil and then drew a circle around a stretch of the river.

"This is my favorite area. And here's where I like to stand in each spot," he said, adding little x's to the map on various sides of the river.

I was dumbfounded. I'm guessing you can relate since you know how we anglers, even the nice ones among us, speak in ambiguities. We answer the question, "What are they biting on?" with statements like, "The end of my line." To the question, "Where'd you catch him?" we reply, "In the river."

Most anglers I've met are cagey about their favorite fishing haunts, but not Scott. The man who had just given me an overview of the sport had now detailed on a map his favorite places to fish.

What's more, as we said goodbye, Scott handed me the map, a net, and two of his rods, reels, and fly boxes.

"Don't worry about losing flies. It'll give me an excuse to tie more," he said.

Scott's generosity illustrates one of the most beautiful aspects of God: He exists in a generous, self-giving relationship. While He is one God, He is three distinct persons: the Father, the Son, and the Holy Spirit. For all eternity, these three persons have continually loved one another. This is why the apostle John doesn't merely write "Love is from God" but also "God is love" (1 John 4:7b, 8b). God is love because He is three persons who, for all time, in all moments, enjoy giving themselves to one another.

This helps us understand the gospel. The gospel is the good news of God generously sending His Son to us. The Father didn't send Jesus to earth to create a religion or give us cold theological truths. He sent His Son because He loves us and wants us to enjoy the Son as He enjoys His Son. The Son, also loving and generous, accomplishes our salvation through the cross so that we can enjoy the Father the way He enjoys His Father. This is why the Father and the Son give us the Spirit of God: so that we can, from spiritually alive hearts, experience a relationship with our triune God for all eternity.

We see this love and selfless generosity in what Jesus prays before enduring the shame of the cross. In John 17:25–26, Jesus prays:

> O righteous Father, even though the world does not know you, I know you, and these know that you have sent me. I made known to them your name, and I will continue to make it known, that the love with which you have loved me may be in them, and I in them.

Can you hear our triune God's loving, generous relationship in that prayer? Can you hear the heart of Jesus for you to enjoy a relationship with His Father in these words? This is why the Christian life can't be reduced to a checklist of good works. It's not a set of rules to follow or lines not to cross. The Christian life is knowing and enjoying God because He has generously given Himself to us.

I did go to Colorado that following week. And I did lose a lot of Scott's flies. I also caught a few fish, including an energetic eighteen-inch rainbow. I'd placed myself on one of the x's on Scott's map, and I'd tied on a size 20 ruby red midge that Scott had tied. I placed my strike indicator precisely in the spot he'd directed, and on the second cast, the plastic ball made the tiniest motion—just a quick zip to the side by no more than an inch. I set the hook, let it run, and when the fish tired out, I netted him with Scott's net.

That entire moment was a gift. As I crouched in that freestone river, cradling the trout in the current until it regained its strength, I felt overwhelmed with gratitude. Toward Scott, of course. But, ultimately, toward the One who had created my friend with His image, the capacity to be generous.

QUESTIONS FOR FURTHER REFLECTION:

1. Do you view your Christian life as a relationship with God, or does it seem more like a set of dos and don'ts, rules to be followed, and lines not to cross?
2. Who in your life has displayed surprising generosity toward you and thereby shown you an example of our generous God? What could you do to honor and appreciate the image of God in this person?
3. How can you practice generosity toward the people in your life?

3

MYSTERY AND PARADOX

You can love completely without complete understanding.

Norman Maclean, *A River Runs through It*

Scripture to Read: 2 Timothy 3:14–17; 2 Peter 3:8–18

My first trout nearly ruined my love for fishing. I was eight, and our family was driving home from a camping trip in the Indian Peaks Wilderness area. I'd spent hours that week trying to catch a fish in Monarch Lake, to no avail. So, when my dad spotted a sign along the interstate that read "Trout Haven: Catching a Fish Is Guaranteed," he took the exit.

We parked our Vanagon camper in front of a small office building and went inside, and my dad paid the woman behind the counter for a ticket. A ticket to catch a fish—that should have been our first warning. While waiting for our guide, I scanned Trout Haven's "Trophy Wall." It displayed Polaroid pictures of hundreds of kids whose parents had taken the exit and who were holding the fish the billboard had guaranteed.

A college-aged kid greeted us enthusiastically. He led us out the door and down to a circular plastic-lined pond the size of a swimming pool surrounded by a concrete walking path. The water was clear, and

I glimpsed several trout swimming back and forth a few feet from the bank. They were all big, and they were all precisely the same size.

My guide handed me a pole, put what looked like a tiny brown marshmallow on the hook, and said, "Give it a good cast!"

For the record, I did give it a good cast, but a good cast wouldn't have been necessary. I could have dropped my line inches from the bank and gotten the same result. The second my bobber slapped the water, it bounced a couple of times, then disappeared. The guide cheered, as I'm guessing he'd been coached to do every time a bobber submerged, and I reeled it in. Someone took a Polaroid. And no more than twenty minutes after my dad had taken the exit, we reentered the freeway. A true been-there-done-that-and-have-the-picture-to-prove-it moment. No wonder. No thrill. Only the question, "What in the world just happened?"

The modern man wants to build a pond, stock it with fish he keeps hungry, and then slap the word *guaranteed* on a billboard. The angler, in contrast, is drawn to mystery. The unknown exhilarates.

Modern man doesn't like mystery. Unsolved, unknown, and unpackaged things unsettle him. Mystery makes him anxious and points out what he hasn't mastered. The modern man wants to build a pond, stock it with fish he keeps hungry, and then slap the word *guaranteed* on a billboard.

The angler, in contrast, is drawn to mystery. The unknown exhilarates. What area should I fish? Where should I cast? Should I pull a leech through the deep riffles or drift an imitation mayfly on the top of the water? Should I troll the lake at twenty, fifty, or a hundred feet? Will the bass hit top-water tonight, or should I bounce a Texas rig on the bottom?

Questions like these—ones that can't be wholly answered—make anglers' hearts pound. These questions cause them to linger in fly shops or at the fishing counters of their local sporting goods stores, feeding on scraps of lore dropped by local experts. Mystery and intrigue are why anglers have been known to stand and stare at the current of a river or the surface of a lake, hoping that the water, in a generous moment, might give up its secrets.

It never does, though. Like a wise old grandfather who always keeps a story or game hidden for the next time his grandkids visit, the waters know how to keep us coming back. They keep us wondering, and we love them for it. Anglers aren't unsettled by mystery; we're invigorated by it.

This is what makes fishers uniquely fit for the study of God. Though the Scriptures give us everything we need to be "wise for salvation through faith in Christ Jesus" (2 Tim. 3:15b), they don't tell us everything about God. They don't resolve every mystery. Having just examined the Trinity in the previous devotion, we're freshly reminded of one of the unsolvable paradoxes of God. How is the one true God three distinct persons? The Bible has much to say in response to that question, but it doesn't *remove* the question. And the triune nature of God is just one example. There are many others, such as:

How is Jesus fully God *and* fully human?

How could our unchangeable God *change* when He took on flesh to dwell with us?

How does God's complete, sovereign governance over all things still allow and accommodate our genuine human freedom to choose?

Why is there evil and loss in the world if our sovereign God is always and only good?

After studying and teaching the Scriptures for more than thirty years, I better understand what the Bible says about these issues. I also have a deeper grasp of what the Bible doesn't say. The more I know God's Word, the bigger some mysteries and paradoxes become. There is a great deal that God hasn't revealed to us.

And there is a great deal that our minds cannot comprehend. God is a transcendent being, infinitely above and beyond us. The prophet Isaiah writes, "For as the heavens are higher than the earth, so are my ways higher than your ways and my thoughts than your thoughts" (Isa. 55:9).

We refer to this set of biblical truths as the *incomprehensibility of God*. Herman Bavinck writes,

> God as the object of human knowledge, who can fathom that? How can man know God, the Infinite and Incomprehensible, who can be measured by neither time nor eternity, in whose presence angels cover their faces with their wings, who lives in unapproachable light, and whom no man has seen nor can see?[2]

We will never fully and completely comprehend all there is to know about our infinite God. This should humble us. It should also excite us. Our future with God holds no billboards, manufactured concrete ponds, or starving fish ... just the pleasures of learning new things about our glorious Creator.

QUESTIONS FOR FURTHER REFLECTION:

1. How comfortable are you with the paradoxes and mysteries mentioned in this chapter? As you've walked with Jesus, which of the questions mentioned in this chapter has troubled you the most?
2. How does our pride factor into our desire to study the Scriptures to solve all the problems and paradoxes of God?
3. Are you tired of fishing in Trout Haven? Are you ready to explore uncharted waters?

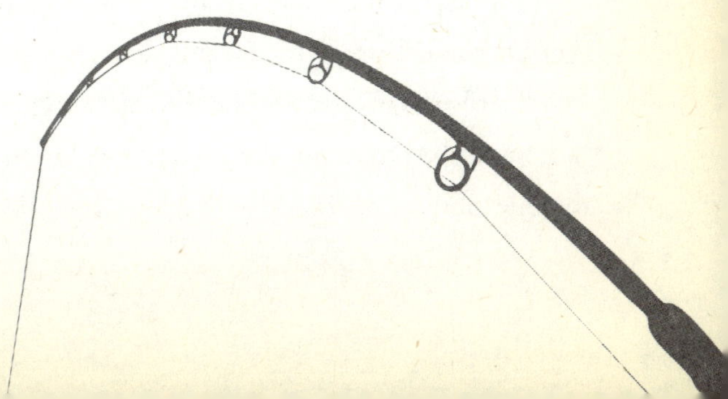

4

ORDER AND LOVE

Rivers and the inhabitants of the watery element were made for wise men to contemplate, and fools to pass by without consideration.

Izaak Walton, *The Compleat Angler*

Scripture to Read: Job 38:8–11; 1 John 5:1–5

The Dream Stream in Colorado gave me one of my best moments as a father. When our kids were the perfect ages for a weeklong camping trip, Jamie and I took them to the mountains southeast of Eleven Mile Canyon. We pitched our tent along Wagon Tongue Gulch Road, not far from a public access spot on the Dream Stream. One morning after a hearty breakfast of pancakes and eggs, Aidan and Claire put on waders and joined me along the bank of the South Platte River. From where we stood, we could see vibrant, healthy trout gulping insects from the water's surface around us.

I'd been to that spot on the Dream Stream several times before, but I felt something different this time. As I looked back from the vast, mighty river to my young children, their tiny frames in oversized waders, a wave of protectiveness washed over me. I leaned my rod against a large boulder and called my kids to my side. I asked Claire to sit on the bank while I walked with Aidan to a safe, shallower spot on the river. I pointed to rocks and underwater structures, giving him a clear set of boundaries for him to respect. I returned for Claire, walking her to another safe and shallow area near her brother. I pointed to a different set of markers and clarified that Claire wasn't to venture farther or deeper.

I knew that stretch of the river. I knew it was a matter of inches between an exhilarating morning of fly fishing and the horrifying experience of trying to find a child swept away by the current. It was a matter of boundaries. I love my children more than life, and the love within my heart made it clear where they could and couldn't fish.

Love and order are not at odds. We see this in the first chapter of the Bible. In Genesis 1, God loves by creating distinction and order. When He begins His work, chaotic waters cover the entire planet. The earth becomes good when, and only when, God sets boundaries for the water. He gives banks to the rivers and shorelines to the ocean. In Job 38:8–11, God asks Job:

> Or who shut in the sea with doors
>   when it burst out from the womb,
> when I made clouds its garment
>   and thick darkness its swaddling band,
> and prescribed limits for it
>   and set bars and doors,
> and said, "Thus far shall you come, and no farther,
>   and here shall your proud waves be stayed"?

It's a popular notion today that to experience joy and life, the self must be unbounded by any constraints or definitions. This is the ideology behind statements like "Don't tell me what sex or gender I am" or "Don't tell me I can't terminate my pregnancy." These are very different issues, yet they are rooted in the same false philosophy that says love and order are contrary.

Yet the Bible teaches that love *provides* order. Love gives definition. Love and order are the essence of all of God's creation, and we will flourish as people only when we live according to the definitions and distinctions God has made. Paul writes this about Jesus in Colossians 1:16b–17: "All things were created through him and for him. And he is before all things, and in him all things hold together."

The Word of God, the preincarnate Christ, created all things. He preexisted all creation, and all creation is sustained by Him today. In displays of His love, Jesus created human bodies male and female, He made the institution of marriage for a husband and a wife, and He created conception and the way vulnerable children grow in their mothers' wombs with purpose, definition, and order. Jesus made us to experience joy, peace, and vibrancy when and only when we live according to His ways. That we doubt His love for us when we read His commands signals our brokenness, not any lack of loving-kindness on His part.

We need only to look at how we love our kids by giving them boundaries to see that God is good and His ways are for our flourishing. That morning on the Dream Stream, my children had no idea of the dangers that the river posed. I did, and I loved them by giving them boundaries. They loved me by keeping them.

Claire and Aidan presented numerous dry flies to those finicky trout from their appointed spots. After an hour of no strikes, a fly (an actual living insect) landed on the top of my hand. It was the tiniest black-bodied, white-winged Trico I'd ever seen. I pulled out my silver fly box, which contained my RS2s, blue-winged olives (BWOs), and the ones that proved to be the heroes of the moment: Tails Up Tricos, one of Landon Mayer's signature flies.

I tied a Tails Up, size 22, onto Claire's 6x tippet and dabbed it with silicone flotant. Claire executed a gentle roll cast upriver. The instant the imitation fly touched the surface of the water, a fish rose and sucked the fly into its mouth. Claire fought it like a champ, and a few moments later, I got to net my daughter's first trout on a fly rod: a beautiful fifteen-inch rainbow.

QUESTIONS FOR FURTHER REFLECTION:

1. Do you see the created order and purpose God gave to the world in Genesis as a good and perfect gift? If so, how does understanding His creation help us know how we should view, treat, and use what He has made?
2. Do you see God's commands in Scripture as limiting your enjoyment or laying out a clear path toward your happiness and well-being?
3. In what ways did your parents, teachers, and coaches give you boundaries as a way of loving and protecting you?

5

KNOWABLE

Hope is like yeast, you know, rising under warmth.

Leif Enger, *Peace like a River*

Scripture to Read: Romans 1:18–23; 1 Corinthians 2:9–15

My wife, Jamie, was pregnant with our first child, Kate, during my last year in seminary. In April, a month before moving from Los Angeles, California, to Ames, Iowa, for me to start work as a college pastor, Jamie and I drove to Huntington Beach. Life was changing quickly, and we wanted to watch the sunset, share a thermos of tea, and talk about becoming parents.

With our feet buried in the sand, I asked Jamie, "What do you most look forward to doing with our children as a mom?"

As the glow of the sunset warmed her cheeks, Jamie described her longing to read her favorite books to our children. Jane Austen, C. S. Lewis, and Lucy Maud Montgomery were a few authors she listed. When she asked me the same question, I described my excitement about taking our kids fishing. When I thought of fatherhood, I thought of times outside, near water, sharing with our children my passion for angling.

Our answers revealed our desire to give ourselves to our children. All loving parents share this heart and vision. We've all received this desire from our Father in heaven, who loves us and desires that we know and receive Him. God wants us to enjoy the things He enjoys. He wants us to know His values, purposes, and priorities. As we discussed in chapter 2, our God has existed as Father, Son, and Spirit for all eternity. He is a relational, generous, and self-giving being. He created us in His image so we would know Him. This doctrine is called the *knowability of God*.

God has expressed Himself so clearly in creation that all humanity encounters Him, Christians and non-Christians alike. In Romans 1, Paul tells us that even those who do not believe in God know Him:

> What can be known about God is plain to them, because God has shown it to them. For his invisible attributes, namely, his eternal power and divine nature, have been clearly perceived, ever since the creation of the world, in the things that have been made. So they are without excuse. For although they knew God, they did not honor him as God or give thanks to him. (vv. 19–21a)

God has shown Himself to everyone by the things He has made. Think of the implications of this: even those who deny that God is real know in their inner being that He is, in fact, real. Paul says that all humankind knows even more than that. Somehow, in some way, everyone understands they have broken God's commands. Paul writes in Romans 1:32, "Though they know God's righteous decree that those who practice such things deserve to die, they not only do them but give approval to those who practice them."

Both those who believe in God and those who do not are alike in that they rightly sense that to break God's decree is to "deserve to die." The knowability of God, conveyed in part through creation, leaves all of us without excuse. We are all aware that God is a command-giver and a just and holy punisher of evil.

For the person saved by grace through faith in Jesus, God's knowability takes on a personal, warm nature. Knowing Him isn't dreadful; it's beautiful. In John 17, Jesus prays for His disciples before going through the cross, grave, resurrection, and ascension. In His prayer, He says, "And this is eternal life, that they know you, the only true God, and Jesus Christ whom you have sent" (v. 3).

The word *know* that Jesus uses in John 17:3 means to know someone *through personal experience*. It means more than simply having the facts straight about that person. It implies that you are in an intimate, familiar relationship with them. When Jesus defines "eternal life" as knowing "the only true God, and Jesus Christ whom [He has] sent," He's describing the joys of being in a relationship with our triune God.

As I write this, that moment on the beach when Jamie and I were drinking tea and dreaming of parenting was twenty-three years ago. All three of our children are now out of the house, either attending college or starting careers. The past two decades were full of reading books and fishing together as a family. Our photo albums contain dozens of pictures of Jamie and me reading to the kids and of the kids holding up bass, walleye, and trout for the camera, joyful smiles sweeping across their faces. We gave them a love both for literature and for great times outside. Most importantly, we gave them ourselves. Like our Father in heaven toward us, we made ourselves known.

My fellow angler, your God wants you to know Him. Like all loving parents, He delights in giving Himself to His sons and daughters. You enter this relationship with God through faith in Jesus. There's nothing you can do to make things right with God; salvation is a gift you receive by trusting in the work of Jesus on the cross. His blood pays for your sins, and He gives His righteousness to you as a gift. If you haven't yet placed your faith in Jesus, I invite you to enter eternal life at this very moment. It's time to know your Father and His Son, Jesus.

The apostle Paul tells us how to do this: "If you confess with your mouth that Jesus is Lord and believe in your heart that God raised him from the dead, you will be saved. For with the heart one believes and is justified, and with the mouth one confesses and is saved" (Rom. 10:9–10).

QUESTIONS FOR FURTHER REFLECTION:

1. What did your father and mother hand down to you because they loved you? What parts of themselves did they most communicate to you?
2. In addition to giving you His Word, what are other ways that your Father in heaven has communicated Himself to you?
3. Herman Bavinck writes, "A knowledge of God is available to man only when, and in so far as, God freely chooses to reveal Himself."[3] Has God made Himself known to you by opening your eyes to the truth of Christ? If so, let me encourage you to pray and give thanks to Him this very moment.

6

THE CORE OF THE UNIVERSE

Time is but the stream I go a-fishing in. I drink at it; but while I drink I see the sandy bottom and detect how shallow it is. Its thin current slides away, but eternity remains.

Henry David Thoreau, *Walden*

Scripture to Read: Romans 8:1–39; 1 John 3:1–3

It's hard to outfish a friend on his own lake. This was certainly the case on a summer afternoon a few years back. Bryan and I were on his boat, working around his pond and mostly celebrating his fish. He easily caught three for each one I hooked. Typically, those types of numbers bug me a bit; I could pretend not to care about who's landing what or how many, but it would be just that—pretending. But that day, I can honestly say that I couldn't have cared less. In fact, at one point, I completely forgot about fishing. It was the moment Bryan told me about his father.

Bryan has been a good friend for nearly thirty years, but this was the first time he had described to me his father's illness and the impact it had had on his childhood. His father spent his days in a hospital bed in their living room for most of Bryan's youth. He had such a severe case of arthritis that he couldn't leave the house for sporting events or family vacations. Their family ate dinner on TV trays in the living room most evenings to be together.

After hearing about this, I expressed my sympathy. My mind raced with thoughts of the losses Bryan had encountered compared to children with physically active fathers. I thought of how my own dad had attended my swim meets, taught me to pitch a baseball, and wrestled with me on the living room floor. I felt sorry for Bryan, and that's when he said something that made me forget about fishing, numbers, or scores.

He acknowledged that it had been difficult to watch his dad be in pain, but then he said, "I had it way better than a lot of my friends."

I couldn't imagine what he meant, so I asked him to explain. He described how most of his classmates rarely saw their fathers. Their dads were always at work or on a trip. They were busy with hobbies or on the phone when they were home. Bryan, however, knew that his dad would be there every afternoon when he returned from school. He'd be excited to hear the details of Bryan's day. He was always present to listen, advise, or pray. While nobody would want their father to go through severe arthritis, I could tell that the presence of Bryan's father had shaped my friend's childhood in significant ways.

God created fathers to be present, positive fixtures in the home. This is proved by the joy we feel when it happens and the grief we encounter when it doesn't. The priority of fatherhood in a home finds its basis in the fatherhood of God. Before anything was created, God was a Father with a Son. The fatherhood of God isn't merely a metaphor or illustration. It is who He is—a Father—and everything He does springs from His fatherly heart. C. S. Lewis, commenting on George MacDonald, writes:

> Far the most important thing we can know about George MacDonald is that … an almost perfect relationship with his father was the earthly root of all his wisdom. From his own father, he said, he first learned that *Fatherhood must be at the core of the universe.* He was thus prepared in an unusual way to teach that religion in which the relation of Father and Son is of all relations the most central.[4]

Many people are interested in God but aren't drawn to Him. They want to escape His judgment and wrath but don't feel the desire to run into His arms as the Prodigal Son entered his father's embrace. How we view God impacts how we feel about Him. If we think of God mainly as creator or judge, our hearts will lack the enthusiasm we should feel.

Jesus longs for us to know His Father as our Father. When someone asked Jesus how to pray, Jesus instructed him to begin with "Our Father in heaven" (Matt. 6:9b).

Think about what Jesus teaches us in those first two words: "Our Father." He wants us to see ourselves as sons and daughters of God. He desires that our intimacy with *our Father* frame our entire prayer life. In *Delighting in the Trinity*, Michael Reeves writes, "Knowing God as our Father not only wonderfully gladdens our view of him; it gives the deepest comfort and joy. The honor of it is stupefying."[5]

Another way to see the centrality of the fatherhood of God is to observe Satan's hatred toward the relationship between the Father and the Son. When Satan tempted Jesus in the wilderness, he did so by trying to disrupt Jesus' devotion to His Father. He addressed Jesus as God's Son to attack the bond Jesus had with His Father. Consider the first temptation: "The tempter came and said to him, 'If you are *the Son of God*, command these stones to become loaves of bread'" (Matt. 4:3).

Jesus responded to Satan's temptations by trusting His Father's words. The Father and Son's love for one another was too sweet to forsake. Jesus replied, "It is written, 'Man shall not live by bread alone, but by every word that comes from the mouth of God'" (v. 4).

Though bested in the wilderness, Satan didn't quit attacking the fatherhood of God and the sonship of Jesus. Throughout Jesus' earthly ministry, the Devil stirred the hearts of religious leaders against Him. What issue did Satan use to offend? The same one: Jesus calling Himself "the Son of God." John records, "This was why the Jews were seeking all the more to kill him, because not only was he breaking the Sabbath, but he was even calling God his own Father, making himself equal with God" (John 5:18).

Because Jesus wouldn't deny His sonship, the religious leaders manipulated the Roman officials into crucifying Him. Three days later, God the Father raised His Son from the dead, proving that not even the powers of hell or the wickedness of humanity can threaten the eternal, loving relationship between the Father and His Son.

Paul describes this permanent, untouchable union that Christians have with the Father through the Son:

> I am sure that neither death nor life, nor angels nor rulers, nor things present nor things to come, nor powers, nor height nor depth, nor anything else in all creation, will be able to separate us from the love of God in Christ Jesus our Lord. (Rom. 8:38–39)

Jesus' life, death, and resurrection redeemed us to our God. Thanks to the Son, we now have our Father. He's always present. He's always eager to listen, teach, and encourage His children. He's never too busy, never distracted, never inaccessible. His sons and daughters matter too much to Him.

I saw an image of this type of father in Bryan's description of his dad. And though I didn't leave the lake with bragging rights, I drove away with something far more valuable: a picture of the power of a present father.

I'll take vision over fish any day.

(But I prefer both, if you let me choose.)

QUESTIONS FOR FURTHER REFLECTION:

1. Did the home in which you grew up talk about knowing God as a Father? Explain your answer.
2. What are ways that your mother and father helped you picture God in a biblically accurate manner? Has the way you were taught about God as a child caused misconceptions about the Father, Son, and Holy Spirit?
3. Are you interested in a deeper examination of God as our perfect Father? If so, I recommend reading my friend Bryan's book, *God's Not Like That: Redeeming Inherited Beliefs and Finding the Father You Long For.*

7

THE WORD

It's also interesting that thoughts about fishing are often carried on in dialogue form where Hope and Fear—or, many times, two Fears—try to outweigh each other.

Norman Maclean, *A River Runs through It*

Scripture to Read: John 1:1–14; Colossians 1:15–20

The fish didn't do what I commanded, or I would have impressed my wife. Years ago, I convinced Jamie to spend a morning in a chair alongside a river watching me fish. We've been married for almost three decades now, but I'm still the young suitor seeking to impress his girl. She knows that, and she's occasionally willing to play along. That morning was one of those occasions, so she brought a chair and a book to the stretch of Pine Creek where I planned to fish. Always the optimist, I entered the river thinking, *Fifteen to twenty fish would be an impressive number. She'd think I was great if I landed that many.*

After two hours of casting without a strike, I revised my hopes downward to five to ten. A fruitless hour later, they were down to three or four. When Jamie mentioned she was returning to the cabin, I just wanted one. That's when I stated my will out loud.

"Come on, fish! Take my fly!"

I repeated some variation of that statement with each cast for the next fifteen minutes. I altered my tone, sometimes trying to sound powerful and in command, at others pleading and begging like the desperate husband I was. I resorted to making deals, like, "Okay, little guys, I'll stop fishing for the day if one of you takes one for the team."

No matter what I said or how I said it, my words held no power. I could see the fish. They were there, just a few feet from where I stood. Their disregard added insult to my defeat. I exited the water a humbled suitor, the all-too-frequent result of my attempts to impress.

Only one Being can make things happen by the power of His words. Hebrews 11:3 tells us, "By faith we understand that the universe was created by the word of God, so that what is seen was not made out of things that are visible."

God didn't start His creative work with preexisting materials. He created all things out of nothing, and He did it by speaking. God spoke, and His Word went forth and accomplished everything He said. Throughout the Old Testament, the words of God directed, sustained, and taught His people.

In the New Testament, John describes the mind-blowing moment in history when this Word of God "became flesh and dwelt among us" to communicate God to us even more personally (John 1:14a). Hebrews 1:1–2a says, "Long ago, at many times and in many ways, God spoke to our fathers by the prophets, but in these last days he has spoken to us by his Son."

As the Word of God accomplished His Father's will in creation, so also Jesus, the incarnate Word of God, accomplished His Father's will in the *new* creation. Through Jesus' life, death, and resurrection, He accomplished God's plan to make all things new. This is why Paul declares that "if anyone is in Christ, he is a new creation" (2 Cor. 5:17a).

The Bible, the written Word of God, continues to make God known and express God's will throughout all generations. We should approach the Scriptures with the same reverence we carry toward God Himself. In John 15:9–10, Jesus equates His words with His very being: "As the Father has loved me, so have I loved you. Abide in my love. If you keep my commandments, you will abide in my love, just as I have kept my Father's commandments and abide in his love." To live according to His words is to abide in Him.

Just as Jesus, the incarnate Word of God, deserves our holy reverence and joyful subordination, so do His words divinely recorded in the Bible. In Psalm 119, the psalmist describes his relationship to God's Word using strong emotional phrases that one would expect a person to use in describing their relationship with God. For example, the psalmist writes, "Your law is my delight" (v. 77b), "Oh how I love your law" (v. 97a), and "I long for your commandments" (v. 131b). He reveres the Scriptures because they're God's words. They are God's self-revelation to us, and thus they command our obedience. Augustine writes, "So for the time being treat the scripture of God as the face of God. Melt in front of it."[6]

The Word of God is divinely authoritative for Christians and non-Christians alike. When we share the gospel, someone may respond, "That's great for you—but that's not my truth. Jesus isn't my God." Yes, He is. If what Christians believe is true, the Word of God *is* their truth. The Word of God created them, sustains them, and will be the judge of all their deeds. This is one of the reasons we must courageously share the gospel. We love people and want them to know and enjoy the One who has communicated clearly and lovingly through His Word.

When I returned to the cabin, Jamie had two plates prepared, and we had lunch together on the porch overlooking the river. My thoughts turned from discouragement to gratitude as I considered two things. First, I'm not Jamie's suitor. As evidenced by the ring on her finger, I had her heart already. My second realization was that it's good that God alone has the power to speak and have His will be done. We hope to see His purposes, not ours, accomplished. And our hope will not be disappointed. God's Word consistently achieves the end for which He sends it, as He said through the prophet Isaiah:

> For as the rain and the snow come down from heaven
> and do not return there but water the earth,
> making it bring forth and sprout,
> giving seed to the sower and bread to the eater,
> so shall my word be that goes out from my mouth;
> it shall not return to me empty,
> but it shall accomplish that which I purpose,
> and shall succeed in the thing for which I sent it.
> (55:10–11)

QUESTIONS FOR FURTHER REFLECTION:

1. When do you most feel frustrated by your lack of power to make your will happen?
2. Does the idea that God's Word never returns empty but always accomplishes His purposes encourage you? How does that certainty give you hope?
3. Do you approach God's Word as if you're listening to God, in person, speaking to you about His plans and purposes? If so, how can you be mindful to do that even more?

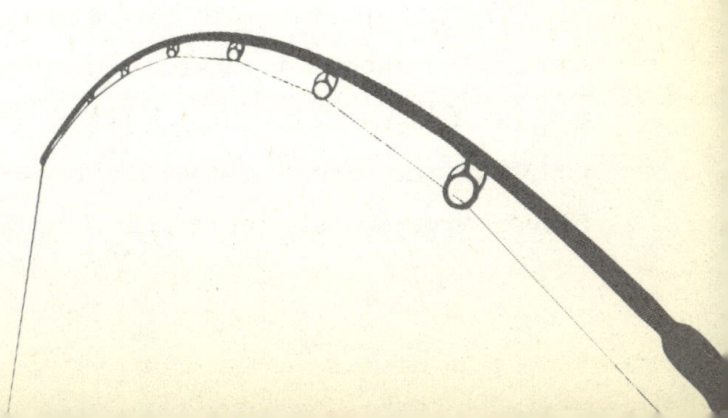

8

IMAGE

You are killing me, fish, the old man thought. But you have a right to. Never have I seen a greater, or more beautiful, or a calmer or more noble thing than you, brother.

Ernest Hemingway, *The Old Man and the Sea*

Scripture to Read: Genesis 1:26–27; Romans 5:12–21

I have a Montana travel poster hanging on the wall of my office. It pictures an angler in the narrow, rocky Stillwater River north of Yellowstone. He's in the moment of truth. The tip of his fly rod is bent like a circle hook, and his line is tight. A monster cutthroat is in mid-jump at the end of the tippet, an imitation blue-winged olive hooked in his bottom jaw. My daughter Claire painted the poster for me, and she, like all skilled artists, can capture movement even in a two-dimensional painting. When I gaze at it, I can see the trout's head and body shaking as he tries to dash the angler's hopes.

I may see movement partly because that's what I remember. I was that angler. I stood in that stretch of the river, my rod bent over by a gorgeous Yellowstone cutthroat. I took pictures of the river, the fish, and even the sky that day. When Claire asked what I wanted for my birthday a couple of months after returning from Montana, I gave her those photos and asked her to work her magic. She might have been a bit charitable with the size of the trout in her painting, but it seems that painters, like angler storytellers, must be granted a generous amount of artistic license.

As with all good art, the beauty of that painting lies in how it directs my thoughts beyond the work itself. That painting depicts a wild and rugged freestone river near Nye, Montana. If you were to wander into my office, you could appreciate the artistic quality of the work, but to truly understand the image, you'd need to visit the Stillwater for yourself. To learn about the image, one must study its subject.

God tells us in Genesis 1:26–27 that He made us in His image. This means we can rightly understand our existence only when we study the being of God. We can enjoy being human, but to rightly understand our value and purpose, we must study the Subject we represent. John Calvin stated this well in Book 1 of his *Institutes*: "No man can survey himself without forthwith turning his thoughts towards the God in whom he lives and moves."[7]

So, who is this God in whose image we were created? The creation narrative tells us He is a generous being who causes people and places to flourish and "swarm with swarms of living creatures" (Gen. 1:20b). He is a relational being, as we see in Genesis 1:26a when He says, "Let *us* make man in our image." "Us" signals the intimate relationship and dialogue between the Father, Son, and Spirit.

When we study God to learn about ourselves, we see that we were created to be good and generous to all creation. Genesis 1:26b reads, "Let them have dominion over the fish of the sea and over the birds of the heavens and over the livestock and over all the earth and over every creeping thing that creeps on the earth." As image bearers, men and women are to steward and cultivate all of God's creation so that people and places flourish.

To be made in God's image also means we're relational. He made us to enjoy being with others and giving ourselves to others. Indeed, husbands and wives giving themselves to one another is how we fulfill the first mandate to "be fruitful and multiply" (Gen. 1:28b).

The image of God in humanity teaches us that every single person has inherent value and dignity. It also shows us that humanity is distinct from all other creatures; our value and our purpose are different. People alone represent and "image" God. God intends humanity to draw creation's gaze to its Creator.

This is one of the reasons some Christian traditions believe that God doesn't want us to make images that represent Him—He's given creation the one image He wants to provide: humanity. You are to draw my eyes to our glorious Creator, and I am to summon your attention to His infinite beauties.

You might object, "Wait, Zeke—you're sinful. You don't image God perfectly."

You'd be right. *Really* right!

Understanding how God created us in His image helps us see our need for Jesus. In Genesis 3, when Adam and Eve disobeyed God's command, they chose to live for themselves instead of their Creator. They decided to seek their own beauty and glory instead of directing creation to see the beauty and glory of God.

When Adam, the first human and representation of us all, sinned, we all sinned. Romans 5:12 says, "Therefore, just as sin came into the world through one man, and death through sin, and so death spread to all men because all sinned." This is why the Bible declares that we are all born "dead in [our] trespasses and sins" (Eph. 2:1b). We're all created in the image of God, but we're also all born in Adam. And as our first human father did, we all start out seeking our glory and greatness instead of God's.

But with the heart of a parent toward a wayward child, our God still loved us. He loved us so much that He sent His Son to rescue us. Paul writes, "God shows his love for us in that while we were still sinners, Christ died for us" (Rom. 5:8).

God intends humanity to draw creation's gaze to its Creator.

Jesus showed us how a human being perfectly lives out the image of God. By flawlessly representing His Father, He gave creation a chance to see its Creator. More than that, He gave creation the gift of being reconciled to its Creator. Where we failed as God's image bearers, Jesus succeeded. The consequence for our sins—death—Jesus paid on the cross. We can't earn our salvation through Jesus. We must receive it as a gift, as Paul writes, "The wages of sin is death, but the free gift of God is eternal life in Christ Jesus our Lord" (Rom. 6:23).

We who have received eternal life in Christ can now "put on the new self, which is being renewed in knowledge after the image of its creator" (Col. 3:10). We can now grow in our ability to image God and direct others to see their Creator. The Spirit of God does this slow and steady work of making us more like Jesus. Our sanctification, just as our salvation, is a gift. We receive this grace as we receive eternal life: by faith.

To become paintings on the wall of this world that point all creation to the beauties of its Creator, we follow Jesus. In every moment of every day, we make His ways ours.

QUESTIONS FOR FURTHER REFLECTION:

1. When you consider the words and deeds of Jesus in the Gospels, what does He show you about the character and personality of God?
2. Which of Jesus' qualities do you most focus on as you prayerfully seek to become more like our Savior, the "image of the invisible God" (Col. 1:15a)?
3. Who in your life represents God well, helping you reflect on the Lord while you're around them?

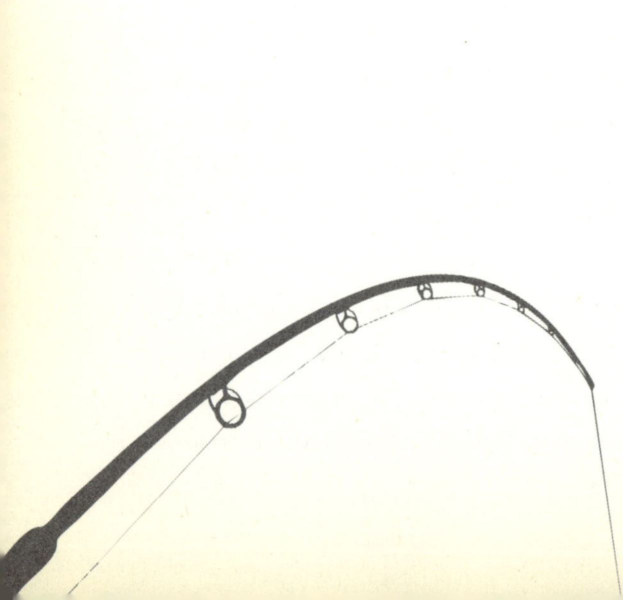

9

COMPANIONS, NOT COMPETITION

Love is like ... a trout stream. Try to capture a trout stream with a dam and you get a lake; try to catch it in a bucket and you get a bucket of water; try to stick some under a microscope and you get a close-up look at some writhing amorphous microcooties. A trout stream is only a trout stream when it's flowing between its own two banks, at its own pace, in its own sweet way.

David James Duncan, *The River Why*

Scripture to Read: 1 Peter 3

Rather than exchange blows, they got married. In David James Duncan's novel *The River Why*, Gus Orviston's parents, Ma and H2O, met in a fabled way. Ma was a bait fisherwoman who dressed like a cowboy. H2O (Henning Hale-Orviston) was a snobbish fly fisherman who wore tweed on the water.

As Gus's uncle, Ma's younger brother, tells the story, Ma and H2O met while H2O was hooked into a massive steelhead. While fighting the fish, a skinny cowpoke dropped into the fishing hole and cast his line across H2O's. When the enormous weight, hook, and worm slapped the water, it spooked the steelhead, and H2O lost his fish of a lifetime.

H2O was livid. Not knowing that the cowboy was a cowgirl—Ma's long hair had been tucked up under her Stetson—H2O picked up a branch, waded toward the intruder, and informed him that he was coming over to fight.

"So be it, Slicker," said the cowpoke.

If God had addressed Adam's loneliness by giving him a couple of male fishing buddies, Eden would have contained three lonely men.

When Ma exited the water, she took off her Stetson, "an' a long braid o' pretty blond hair fell from under the hat."[8] H2O's jaw, and the stick he was carrying, dropped to the ground. The two made a campfire and then, shortly after, got married. They got along just fine that first night. The rest of the novel, however, describes one verbal fisticuff after another. This bait fisher and fly angler were opposed to each other in every possible way.

This is not the vision the Bible gives us of men and women. In Genesis 1, God's creative work involved taking a chaotic place and giving it order and distinction. The earth was without form and void, but when God had finished His work, it teemed with life.

The goodness of God's work can be seen in how He created *complementary pairs*—two-isms—that work perfectly well together. He separates the sky from the land; they're both good, and they both serve vital purposes. Likewise, He distinguishes the livestock from wild animals. The sun has its time and place, and the moon and stars have theirs. These two-isms work together, not against each other. Both sides are equally vital to creation's flourishing.

The crowning jewel of two-isms in the creation narrative is the gift of Eve for Adam. Genesis 1 and 2 present the unity and equality of men and women, as well as their complementary distinctions. As we discussed in the previous devotion, both men and women were made in God's image. They are both essential and vital in God's created purpose for humanity. They were both blessed by God and given the commandment: "Be fruitful and multiply and fill the earth and subdue it, and have dominion over the fish of the sea and over the birds of the heavens and over every living thing that moves on the earth" (Gen. 1:28b).

Any worldview or religion that presents men as more important or superior to women is wrong, according to God's Word. What's more, any movie, sitcom, commercial, or social movement that suggests that the two sexes are fundamentally in competition—and for one to get ahead, the other must fall behind—is unbiblical. The most essential reality about us as male and female is sameness. This is the focus of Genesis 1.

In Genesis 2, the focal point shifts to the *otherness* of women and men. The distinctions, too, are good and holy. God created Eve differently. The timing and process of her creation were different from

Adam's, as was her physiology. In Genesis 2:18, when it's just Adam, God declares that things aren't good yet. There is a remaining work, something yet for God to create if humanity is to be all He intends us to be.

God lets Adam experience this not-good state for himself when He gives Adam the task of naming all the other two-isms—perfect, complementary companions—in creation. Adam sees that every creature has a companion and that both are essential to fruitfulness. Through that task, Adam joins God in knowing that something is missing: a partner who would not only remove his loneliness but would also make humanity's fruitfulness possible.

God puts Adam to sleep and takes a rib from his side to create Eve. That He put Adam to sleep signals that Eve's creation is God's work. She is His gift to Adam. And what a gift she is! Her body, mind, soul, and spirit are the perfect counterpart to Adam's. Males and females are the same—they share the human nature—yet they are the most brilliant two-ism in the world. Their distinctions as well as their similarities display the image of God to creation. "So God created man in his own image, in the image of God he created him; male and female he created them" (Gen. 1:27).

It had to be Eve. Men had to have women. If God had addressed Adam's loneliness by giving him a couple of male fishing buddies, Eden would have contained three lonely men. Sure, they may have enjoyed fishing the no-doubt pristine, salmon-packed rivers of Eden. But they would have spent their nights commiserating by a campfire, their lonely tears extinguishing the flames before returning to their shelters to sleep alone.

Women are a gift from God to men, and men are a gift from God to women. Like Ma and H2O, we may choose different forms of fishing, and that's fine. What's important is that we view one another as companions, not competitors.

QUESTIONS FOR FURTHER REFLECTION:

1. What married couple in your life best displays the companionship God intends for a husband and wife?
2. Do your friendships with the opposite sex illustrate how men and women are equal yet distinct in essential ways? If not, what can you change so that you honor the Lord in how you relate to your opposite-sex friends?
3. What are ways that our society promotes unbiblical, hurtful pictures of relationships between husbands and wives and between men and women in general?

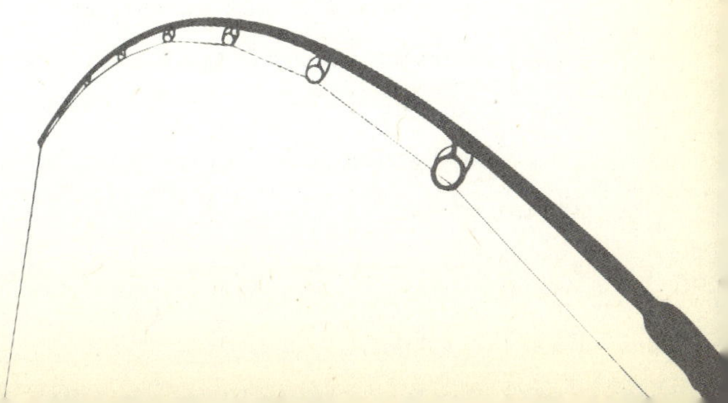

10

IT JUST TAKES ONE

There is no activity so conducive to the health and happiness of a civilized man as angling with an artificial fly. As for the uncivilized, who would care to contemplate what writhing creatures their inchoate consciences allow them to skewer upon a hook?

David James Duncan, *The River Why*

Scripture to Read: 1 Corinthians 10:11–13; Ephesians 6:10–20

In the summer of 2021, I spent a week fly fishing the Savage River in northwest Maryland. The cobblestoned river runs along the bottom of a steep valley. Forested hillsides rise quickly from both banks. Hemlocks, oaks, and elms stand true and tall, their limbs stretching out to provide a protective canopy over the dapple-lighted river below.

I tried all my favorite flies that first morning but couldn't get a strike. Scuds, RS2s, San Juan worms, and midges, but nothing worked. With a few hours of daylight remaining, I did what every befuddled angler would do: I drove to the closest fly shop and tried to become best friends with the owner.

When I arrived, Paul was sweeping river dirt off the stoop beside the front door.

Before I could say a word, he said, "Let me guess ... you're not catching anything?"

"So, it's not just me then?" I replied.

Paul explained how every person fishing the Savage that week had shuffled their wader boots across his parking lot and through his front door in the same defeated manner. I admit that hearing I wasn't alone lifted my spirits. Misery loves company.

"They've got eyes for one thing this week, and nothing else will do," Paul said. "They only want cicadas."

My time on the Savage coincided with the seventeen-year Brood X cicada hatch. I knew this, of course. These insects are incredibly loud. Their high-pitched, undulating sounds can reach one hundred decibels, the loudness of a lawnmower. I also knew this because, while driving from the airport to the river, I had to stop numerous times to wash the black-and-orange gelatinous remains of these bugs off the windshield of my rental car. Yes, I knew of the hatch. It just hadn't occurred to me that the trout were eating these giant bugs.

Nothing in my fly box mimicked cicadas. I scanned the flies in the display by the cash register, but nothing in the plastic bins looked like cicadas either. I must have looked desperate because when I looked back at Paul, he held up his index finger and disappeared into a back room. He emerged a moment later carrying a single perfect top-water imitation of a Brood X cicada.

"It's my only one," he said, "so tie your knots carefully."

That I did. For four days, I fished with strong tippet, retied often, and netted dozens of brown and rainbow trout. It took one and only one imitation of the real thing to fool those fish over and over again.

Jesus tells us that we have an enemy who seeks to steal, kill, and destroy our sweet communion with God (see John 10:10a). In Ephesians 6:11, the apostle Paul writes, "Put on the whole armor of God, that you may be able to stand against the schemes of the devil." The apostle Peter tells us the same thing: "Be sober-minded; be watchful. Your adversary the devil prowls around like a roaring lion, seeking someone to devour" (1 Pet. 5:8).

Like me on the Savage River, Satan needs only one fly in his box, one imitation of the real thing. His strategy is to try to get us to doubt God's provision and the truthfulness of His Word. For example, when God commanded Adam to not eat the fruit of the Tree of Knowledge of Good and Evil (Gen. 2:17), that boundary was a good gift. God was not playing games or being tricky. He wasn't holding back something special. Through the command, God provided Adam and Eve the opportunity to enjoy obedience to their Creator.

Satan tempted Eve by calling into question God's words to her, causing her to wonder whether God was actually providing everything Adam and Eve needed. In Genesis 3, he twists—deceptively imitates—God's words by asking Eve a question: "Did God actually say, 'You shall not eat of any tree in the garden'?" (v. 1b).

Satan knew that God hadn't told Adam and Eve they couldn't eat from *any* tree in the garden. The question employed a lie. The Father of Lies created doubts in Eve's mind. *Could it be that God wants to limit my knowledge and happiness? Perhaps God isn't entirely for my welfare? Are there things that He's keeping from me?*

Eve responds by quoting the words of God, but she also changes them when she adds this bit: "Neither shall you touch it" (v. 3b).

Satan responds with another lie meant to make Eve doubt God's truthfulness. "The serpent said to the woman, 'You will not surely die. For God knows that when you eat of it your eyes will be opened, and you will be like God, knowing good and evil'" (vv. 4–5).

Satan carries a tiny fly box. It needs to be large enough to house only one fly. He tempted Jesus with this same strategy, and he still uses it today. He knows that if he can take our eyes off God's perfect love, His provision, and the truthfulness of His words, we'll take things into our hands.

The Christian life can sometimes feel overwhelming because it seems like our enemy is attacking us with complicated, varied strategies. He's not, though. It's all one fly. The core issue in any temptation is this: Is God perfectly loving in all He provides?

We may struggle with the temptation to view pornography. We may desire to lie to protect ourselves or present ourselves in a good light. We may feel a strong pull toward using food, drugs, or alcohol as an escape from feelings of pain, fear, or shame. We may struggle with all three of those categories and several others. The Christian life can sometimes feel overwhelming because it seems like our enemy is attacking us with complicated, varied strategies.

He's not, though. It's all one fly. The core issue in any temptation is this: Is God perfectly loving in all He provides? Can His words be trusted completely?

Take the temptation to view pornography as an example. In the moment of desire, we face the choice of believing something true or false about God. Is God in favor of your vibrancy and flourishing as a sexual being? Are all His commands regarding sexual ethics and fleeing immorality keeping you from things that would make you happier? Will choosing to sin bring more life and peace to your inner being than believing God's Word?

Satan plants those questions in our minds and suggests lies for their answers. His goal is to draw our focus away from God's loving provision and toward the things we want. His goal is to encourage us to trust in our desires and determinations instead of God's Word. He drops this fly ever so gently onto the water's surface just above our eyes. He'll twitch it, try to make it look alive and real. He wants us to bite without noticing that his fly has a huge barbed hook protruding from the abdomen. His aim is our misery, as the Puritan Thomas Brooks writes:

> His first Device to draw the soul to sin, is, to present the bait, and hide the hook; to present the golden cup, and hide the poison; to present the sweet and the pleasure, that may flow into the soul by yielding to sin, and hide from the soul the wrath and misery that will certainly follow the committing of sin.[9]

To stand against the Devil, we must believe that God is always good and always faithful. What He brings into our lives or takes out of them is always His perfect provision. We must read the Scriptures with the prayerful aim of trusting every command and promise. We must let the imitation drift right on by so we can delight in the real thing—as the psalmist describes: "Oh, taste and see that the LORD is good! Blessed is the man who takes refuge in him!" (Ps. 34:8).

While fishing the Savage River, I took a picture of the Brood X cicada imitation next to a real cicada that had landed on a moss-covered rock along the bank. I tip my hat to the person who tied that fly—except for the hook, it looks identical to the real thing. When I'm tempted toward this sin or that one, I often pull up that photo on my computer. It reminds me that our enemy knows the truth accurately enough to imitate it deceptively well. It also warns me that one option nourishes, and the other just flat-out hurts.

QUESTIONS FOR FURTHER REFLECTION:

1. What is the lie Satan presents to you often? When you look at the sins you most often commit, what falsehoods do you believe about God that fuel your choices to disobey Him?
2. How have your sins—the hook protruding from the belly of the fly—hurt you or those around you?
3. Read 1 John 1:9–10. How do confession and repentance lead to an appetite for the real thing instead of the deceitful, false imitations Satan presents? What role does God's mercy play in your desire to be faithful?

11

DAMAGED

Do unto those downstream as you would
have those upstream do unto you.

Wendell Berry, *Citizenship Papers: Essays*

Scripture to Read: John 3:16–21; James 4:1–10

"Excuse me, sir, but you're fishing too close to me."

A young man made that comment to me a couple of summers ago when I waded into Lake Taneycomo near the fish hatchery. The young man was correct: I'd walked to within ten feet of where he'd been fishing.

The outlet from the hatchery creates a strong current, and the trout in that system like to stack up in the seam where the fast water and slow water meet. This young angler knew that, which is why he'd gotten up earlier than anyone else to snag that position. I was an interloper, an intruder. My self-centeredness had been in such a feeding frenzy that it had overpowered my social decency. I'd slipped inappropriately into the young man's casting lane. To his credit, he'd been patient; he commented only after I'd crossed his line and knotted us up.

Not only was his statement accurate, but it was also convicting. I had made that precise comment to an angler who had crowded me when I was in the very same sweet spot a decade before. About ten years earlier, I'd been the young man who had gotten up early to claim that perfect casting spot. I'd been the one who'd had an older angler slip into the water midmorning and walk to within ten feet of where I was fishing. It was my fishing line that had gotten crossed, creating a knot that had taken me five minutes to untie.

In Genesis 1–2, we learn that creation as God made it is good. Adam and Eve, representatives of all humanity, began their lives properly oriented toward God. Their hearts and minds were focused on the beauties of their Creator and each other's well-being. A person in a proper relationship with God is delighted by doing good things for others.

Our sin is a big deal. It reorients us, turning us from the desire to glorify God and serve people. Our sin fixes our hearts on getting what we want. People become obstacles or opportunities. They're obstacles when they're in the job, leadership position, or fishing spot that you want to be in. They are opportunities when they can enhance your reputation, write a reference letter, or give you directions to the best fishing spots on the river. If we view people as either obstacles or opportunities, we can know that in our minds we've turned them into objects to advance our selfish wants.

The Old Testament is filled with painful, wicked events: war, rape, families torn apart, deaths by the thousands. Sadly, we still see these awful things happening today. As terrible as these actions are, they're not the core issue. They are symptoms. The root cause of all cruelty is a heart that views people as tools, resources, and things to use for our wants. David Foster Wallace made a confession during a commencement address in 2005, saying,

> Here's one example of the utter wrongness of something I tend to be automatically sure of. Everything in my own immediate experience supports my deep belief that I am the absolute center of the universe, the realest, most vivid and important person in existence. We rarely think about this sort of natural, basic self-centeredness, because it's so socially repulsive, but it's pretty much the same for all of us, deep down. It is our default setting, hardwired into our boards at birth. Think about it: There is no experience you've had that you were not at the absolute center of.[10]

Wallace's confession was not only refreshingly honest but also theologically accurate. The human heart infected by sin orients a person's entire world around self, as James writes, "Where jealousy and selfish ambition exist, there will be disorder and every vile practice" (3:16).

If *self* is the problem, then expecting our *self* to fix things is foolish. Only Christ's power in us can free us from selfishness. The gospel is the message that Jesus humbled Himself and became human. He lived a perfect, righteous life, always honoring His Father and loving His neighbor. He was never selfish, and He never sinned. As the only innocent person to walk the face of the earth, Jesus could be our substitute, and He died a criminal's death in our place. His life and His death on the cross are the supreme example of honoring God and putting others first.

The Spirit of God gives us the power to live for the glory of God and the welfare of others. My fellow angler, Christ has set us free from self so that we can follow His example and keep His command: "You shall love the Lord your God with all your heart and with all your soul and with all your mind. This is the great and first commandment. And a second is like it: You shall love your neighbor as yourself" (Matt. 22:37b–39).

After the young man's comment, I removed my sunglasses so he could see the sincerity in my eyes. I apologized, and I meant it with every bit of my being. I said, "You are absolutely right. I'm embarrassed. I had someone do this to me once ... and I can't believe I did it to you. I'll move downriver."

The young man, gracious in his rebuke, was even kinder in his response. He encouraged me not to go too far, saying, "Perhaps only five more feet; that way, you can still fish this seam."

We fished that area together for the rest of the day, netting each other's fish and celebrating each other's success. We even met the following morning and fished it again.

QUESTIONS FOR FURTHER REFLECTION:

1. Can you remember a time when your selfishness was in a feeding frenzy? How did you treat others?
2. Is there someone you need to go to and ask for forgiveness from because of a moment of selfishness?
3. How does reminding yourself of the gospel each day fuel your desire to be kind and considerate? What passages in the Bible do you read to recall the mercy and grace of God?

12

WATER

Yes, as everyone knows, meditation and water are wedded forever.

Herman Melville, *Moby-Dick*

Scripture to Read: Matthew 8:23–34

It was my favorite fishing trip with my mom and dad, and it took place fifty feet above a small town in Nebraska. When I was nine, my parents drove me three hours west of Lincoln to fish Lake McConaughy. It took us only four hours to catch our limit of white bass, yellow perch, and crappie.

At one point in the evening, our guide said, "If you dropped your line fifty feet down, you'd probably hit the Harrises' old root cellar."

His conversation starter worked. We begged him for the story.

The guide described how Lake McConaughy had been created in 1941 at the expense of the residents of Lemoyne, Nebraska. Lemoyne had been a quaint little town whose only fault was that it was situated in the way of progress. Founded in the early 1880s by Lemoyne Jacobs, the village sat alongside the North Platte River. By the 1930s, Lemoyne boasted a railroad stop, general store, hotel, school, and bank. But when plans for the Kingsley Dam took shape, the authorities evoked eminent domain, forcing the residents to relocate. In 1941, the waters rolled in and covered the structures of the peaceful village, including the Harrises' old root cellar.

Water is a significant theme throughout the Bible's storyline. Rivers, lakes, seas, and storms aren't random, ungoverned features of creation. They point us to God's sovereignty, illustrating both God's judgments and His choices to give mercy and grace.

For example, we see God's power to give life in Genesis 1. When God began His creative work, the earth was covered with water. Water, in that moment, symbolized chaos and a lack of goodness. As God created and ordered the world, He gave the waters boundaries and made them swarm with the fish we love to catch. He also placed four rivers in the garden of Eden as a gift for humanity, symbols of His faithful provision. When God created the human body to consist of 60 percent water, He made us need water. The four rivers in the garden of Eden, along with the river of life in the new heavens and new earth, are symbols of His desire and ability to meet our needs.

Throughout the Old Testament, water continually points to God's faithfulness in giving us life. For example, in Genesis 21, Hagar and her son, Ishmael, were lost in the wilderness. They were about to die of dehydration when God gave them a well. In Exodus 17, after God had led the Israelites out of Egypt, He gave them water through Moses's staff as they moved toward the Promised Land.

These moments teach us about our dependence on God and God's faithfulness to provide. They help us understand the statement that Jesus made to the Samaritan woman who was thirstier for salvation than for water: "Everyone who drinks of this water will be thirsty again, but whoever drinks of the water that I will give him will never be thirsty again. The water that I will give him will become in him a spring of water welling up to eternal life" (John 4:13b–14).

Just as God is faithful to save us from dying of dehydration, He's also able to save us from our most desperate threat: the judgment, wrath, and eternal punishment we deserve because of our sins.

Toward that same end, water is also consistently used to symbolize God's perfect judgment and wrath. In Genesis, when the Lord "saw that the wickedness of man was great in the earth," He caused water to cover the entire earth once again (6:5a). It destroyed all living things except the ones He saved through the ark. During the exodus, God made the Red Sea close upon the Egyptians as judgment for enslaving His people (Exodus 14). And during the earthly ministry of Jesus, God used a lake to judge and remove the demons that Jesus cast out of a man and into pigs (Matthew 8). Water points us not only to God's faithfulness but also to His wrath.

Whether God employs water to give life or execute judgment, the Bible's message is that all forms of water bow to Him. God is supremely in charge of rivers, seas, oceans, and storms. Psalm 135:6 declares, "Whatever the LORD pleases, he does, in heaven and on earth, in the seas and all deeps."

When we understand the symbolism of water, we can see that when Jesus calmed the storm threatening the disciples' lives (see Mark 4:35–41), He displayed how, as God, He had the power to make the waves submit to His words. Jesus can part the waters, give them boundaries, calm them, and walk on them.

He can even dry them up, which He did with the water of Lake McConaughy several years ago.

In 2004, a severe drought in Nebraska caused McConaughy's water levels to drop 80 percent. Many of the descendants of the original Lemoyne residents saw the town once more. Stumps of trees that had lined Main Street jutted a few feet from the sandy soil. They saw the foundations of the gas station and hotel. They even got a glimpse of Arch and Ivy Harris's root cellar.[11]

For us anglers, many of our favorite places involve water. My hope behind this devotion is that you and I will never fish a river, lake, or sea without praising and worshipping God for His sovereign governance over all things. My prayer is that our favorite waters will draw us to repent when we think about the judgment and wrath we deserve and that they will also freshly remind us of the faithfulness of God to give us life through Jesus, His Son.

QUESTIONS FOR FURTHER REFLECTION:

1. In addition to the biblical references in this devotion, can you think of other instances in the Bible in which water points to the judgment or grace of God?
2. How has God used water in your life to remind you of His sovereignty over all creation?
3. What is one body of water that reminds you that God is in control and that He loves to give life and refresh our hearts? What is it about that river, lake, or ocean that humbles you and makes you think of the Lord?

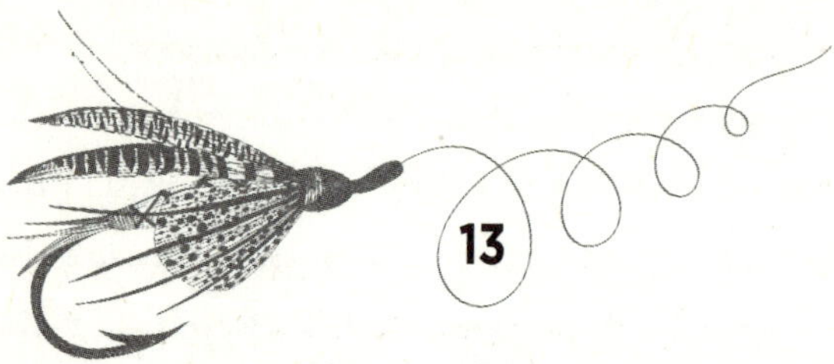

13

CAN DEAD THINGS LIVE?

You keep the early trout (anyone who doesn't is too saintly to be normal) but in time you begin to see the virtue of releasing the wild fish. The logic is infallible: if you kill him, he's gone; if you release him, he's still there.

John Gierach, *Trout Bum*

Scripture to Read: Ezekiel 37:1–10; John 11:17–44

I release *almost* all the trout I catch. I'm not a trout snob who scorns the angler upstream for keeping a good-eatin'-sized fish to prepare for their family. For me, it's an issue of taste and preference more than conviction. I love the taste of salmon, walleye, and perch, but it's a rare mood that makes me want to eat trout. That craving comes along once or twice a year.

That said, there is a bit of conviction at work. I shared John Gierach's quote above because I always think about it. I can say this honestly and with a witness to prove it: a few years back, I caught the same eighteen-inch brown trout out of the same stretch of Fremont Canyon in Wyoming three times in one week. The scar on his cheek just behind his maxillary bone made him quickly recognizable.

To each their own if we're enjoying our sport and respecting the fish we catch. What does bother me is the careless, unnecessary death of a wild trout. Especially a wise old survivor like the twenty-seven-inch rainbow that went stiff in my hands.

I had been fly fishing below Gray Reef Dam when a young man in an old hatchback pulled into the parking lot. When he reached his perch on the dock, he began casting a spoon toward the white waters of the spillway. We waved at each other, and I returned to focusing on my strike indicator. When the sun dropped below the mountains to the west, I exited the river and started a campfire. The young man walked up a few moments later and asked if I wanted to keep a big fish he'd caught.

I wasn't in one of those rare moods when I craved the taste of trout, so I politely declined. He asked me if I wanted to see the fish, describing it as the biggest one he'd ever caught. I followed him back to the dock. A few feet into the water next to the concrete pier, a gigantic rainbow slowly opened and closed its mouth. It was desperately trying to move water over its gills. The boy explained that he never intended to eat it but did want to show it to whoever was around at the end of the day. He was proud of his resourcefulness; he didn't have a stringer, so he'd threaded a piece of rebar jutting from a concrete brick through the trout's gills and out its mouth. He asked again if I'd like to have the fish for dinner.

I'd never caught a trout that big. I've only seen its equal a few times in all my years of fishing. Not only did I not want to keep it, but I wanted it to live. I asked the boy if I could try to revive the fish, and he agreed. I pulled it away from the metal rod, carried it to the current, and held it underwater. I cradled it in my hands and moved it forward so that water passed through its mouth and gills. I pleaded with the fish to swim, but to no avail. It stopped opening and closing its mouth. Its body stiffened like a wet two-by-four.

Death held that fish in its grip long before my hands tried to help. It doesn't matter how badly we want something or someone to live: the dead do not come back to life.

Or do they? In Ezekiel 37, God's Spirit takes the prophet Ezekiel to a desert valley covered with dry human bones. By the time Ezekiel encounters these remains, unlike that trout, they are long dead. That's the message behind the word "dry." Any flesh or hope of living that once remained with these bodies had expired so long ago that the bones were brittle and powdery.

God asks Ezekiel, "Son of man, can these bones live?" (v. 3a).

Ezekiel likely wrestled with two competing thoughts at that moment. On the one hand, he knew what we all know: dead things, especially long-dead things, don't come back to life. But, on the other hand, he knew that he was talking with God, the One who took a lifeless planet and filled it with living things.

Considering these thoughts, Ezekiel's response was wise. "O Lord GOD, you know" (v. 3b).

God commands Ezekiel to preach to the bones. Ezekiel preaches, and as the words of God enter the valley, the bones come together. The words of God put flesh upon them. Then, through Ezekiel, God's words summon the wind and blow life into the long-dead bodies once again.

In Genesis 1, we see that God's word has the power to create and give life. In Ezekiel 37, we see that God's word has the power to *re-create* and give new life. This vision foreshadows the salvation that Jesus, the Word of God made flesh, gives us. Paul presents this same theology in his letter to the Ephesians when he writes, "But God, being rich in mercy, because of the great love with which he loved us, even when we were dead in our trespasses, *made us alive together with Christ*" (2:4–5a).

We are all born dead in our trespasses and sins. Dead is dead, and just as I was powerless to bring that fish back to life, so we are helpless to remove the grip of death from our souls. But the Word of God gives new life to all who believe in Him.

God offers us this new life through the gospel—the preached, written, and communicated good news about what Jesus did for us on the cross. I was nineteen when I heard the gospel, believed, and became a "new creation" (2 Cor. 5:17). Since then, I've had the joy of being in the room dozens of times when the Spirit of God through the Word of God breathed new life into a long-dead heart. God alone makes dead things live.

Has He done this work in your heart, my fellow angler? If not yet, perhaps today is the day.

QUESTIONS FOR FURTHER REFLECTION:

1. Why do you think God involves people like Ezekiel, Paul, you, and me in His work of giving life to dead hearts?
2. Do you go through times when you feel dry and dead inside? If so, how does drawing near to God and relying on His Spirit give you vibrancy and strength?
3. Who are the people you are praying for who need to have their sins forgiven and find new life in Christ?

14

THE INCARNATION

Perhaps I should not have been a fisherman, he thought.
But that was the thing that I was born for.

Ernest Hemingway, *The Old Man and the Sea*

Scripture to Read: Hebrews 2:14–17; 4:14–16

Not all bass fishing is the same, as I discovered a few weeks before writing this. One of my close friends, Matt, has been asking me for several years to fish a particular lake in northern Nebraska. It's a four-hour drive from home, and with a dozen sandpit lakes within ten miles of my back door, I haven't seen the need to travel to catch bass. Each time I've turned Matt down, he's said, "One of these times, you're going to have to trust me. This isn't like other bass fishing."

So one day, I decided to trust Matt. We got up early and made it to the lake by midmorning. We fished from float tubes. We waded from the shallows into the deep, and when we couldn't touch bottom, we sat on the seat straps and paddled our wader boots to move from one spot to another.

A few casts into the outing, it felt like my hook snagged a passing car. The bass slammed my creature bait so hard that it almost jerked the rod from my hands. He didn't tap on the line like most bass. He took my lure to the bottom of the lake and parked the car. I muscled him up, one crank of the bait caster at a time. Matt took a picture, and I put the fish back. I was thrilled and optimistic: I'd caught the first fish of the outing, and we still had five hours of fishing ahead!

For the next five hours, I watched Matt hook, fight, and bring one lunker after another to his tube. I had two, and only two, more strikes that day and didn't land either one. It's one thing if both guys are getting skunked; it's another thing to watch your buddy catch twelve in a row. As we drifted across the lake toward the truck, I felt sorry for myself. Now, I didn't want to feel sorry for myself; it's not an enjoyable frame of mind. Moreover, mopey Zeke isn't a fun travel companion. Matt deserved better on our trek home.

In the fifteen minutes it took to drift into the shallows by the truck, I returned to feeling excited and grateful.

How? What did I think about that turned me around?

It wasn't the thought of outfishing Matt next time, although that's my sincere hope. Instead, it was the idea that our holy God took on flesh and became human. Thinking about the incarnation of Jesus lifted my spirits. Bobbing up and down in a giant rubber tube, I thought about Hebrews 2:14–17, which is a great passage for understanding the incarnation.

Throughout the Old Testament, the radiance of God was so glorious that human beings couldn't see or touch Him and live. When Moses met with the Lord, he "hid his face, for he was afraid to look at God" (Ex. 3:6b). Years later, when Moses wanted to look upon God, the Lord said, "You cannot see my face, for man shall not see me and live" (Ex. 33:20).

The Old Testament is filled with moments displaying the chasm between sinful man and the holy God. When David was bringing to Jerusalem the ark of the covenant—God's dwelling place with Israel—one of the men helping carry the ark touched it and immediately died (2 Samuel 6). First Samuel 6:19 records how seventy men of Beth-shemesh died after looking upon the ark. The men who survived cried out, "Who is able to stand before the LORD, this holy God?" (v. 20b). Throughout the Hebrew Scriptures, no one could see or touch the Lord and live.

And then, one night in the town of Bethlehem, a brand-new mother held this God in her arms. She peered into His eyes. She heard every cry and cooing sound He made. "Mary treasured up all these things, pondering them in her heart" (Luke 2:19).

At the birth of Christ, God made Himself seeable and touchable. He didn't cease being God, but He did become something He hadn't been: human. The God whose face Moses couldn't see now had eyes to gaze into, a mouth that needed food, and a bottom that needed to be wiped.

All who saw Jesus saw God. Herman Bavinck writes, "Christ is the image of God, the brightness of God's glory, and the express image of His person. In Christ the invisible God has become visible. Whoever sees Him sees the Father (John 14:9)."[12]

It wasn't just Mary and Joseph who saw God through Jesus. For the next several years, people from Nazareth watched Him grow and increase "in wisdom and in stature and in favor with God and man" (Luke 2:52b). Friends talked with Him, ate meals with Him, laughed at jokes with Him. Enemies yelled at Him. They mocked Him. They conspired against Him. They condemned Him, crucified Him, and buried Him. And they could do all these things because Jesus humbled Himself and took on flesh. Because of His incarnation.

Like many people, I can focus on what is not going according to my plans and feel discouraged. Over the years, I've found that several truths from God's Word can lift my heart out of any degree of self-pity when I choose to think of them. The incarnation is a potent example of soul-lifting theology.

D. Martyn Lloyd-Jones captures this idea of speaking truth to our hearts in his book *Spiritual Depression*:

> The main art in the matter of spiritual living is to know how to handle yourself. You have to take yourself in hand, you have to address yourself, preach to yourself, question yourself. You must say to your soul; "Why art thou cast down"—what business have you to be disquieted?[13]

My fellow angler, the next time you're getting outfished by a close friend who, like Matt, will quite likely remind you of the final tally for years to come, think upon the incarnation of Christ and see if you stay sad.

I don't think it's possible.

QUESTIONS FOR FURTHER REFLECTION:

1. How does studying creation in Genesis 1 help us understand the incarnation as described in Luke 2 and John 1?

2. What does Hebrews 4:14–16 tell us is the difference between Jesus' humanity and our humanity?
3. Considering Hebrews 4:14–16, how does it benefit us that Jesus, who sits at His Father's right hand, is still fully human (and fully divine)?

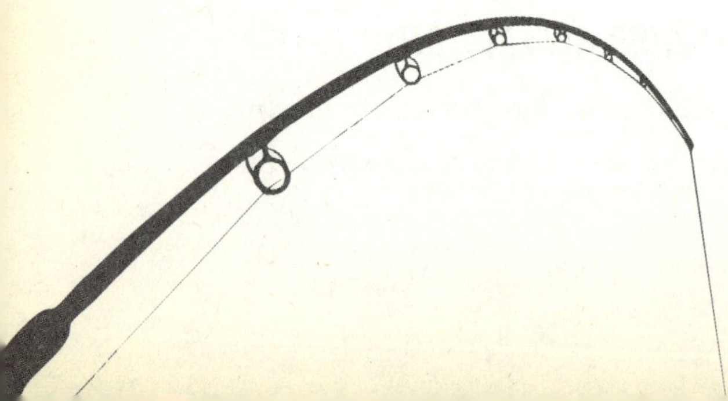

15

NO ONE LIKE HIM

If I can, you can.

Clay Dyer

Scripture to Read: John 6

Some of my favorite athletes are professional bass fishermen. Jay Yelas, my friend who wrote the afterword for this book, is a great example. So is Clay Dyer, another bass pro I've followed throughout the years. Clay started fishing when he was five and began competing when he was fifteen. He fished with Fishing League Worldwide (FLW) from 2000 to 2010 and then with Bass Anglers Sportsman Society (BASS) in 2012. Ask Clay's professional colleagues, and they'll say he's one of the most respectable anglers to have competed in the sport.

He's also one of the most inspiring. The fact that Clay's fishing and boating skills are in the top 1 percent is made more remarkable by the fact that he was born without legs, without an arm on his left side, and with just a partial arm on his right side. Despite those challenges, Clay maintains an upbeat, if not playful, attitude on the water.

Don't get me wrong: he's a competitor. He refuses to use modified gear. He rigs up and casts the same rods and reels that other professional anglers use. He ties knots with his tongue. He casts by squeezing the rod between his jaw and collarbone, then whipping it forward with a quick left-to-right twist of his upper body. When he hooks a fish, he reels it in by placing the butt of the rod under his chin and reeling with his right arm. Once he boats the fish, he unhooks it with his teeth. Clay's motto, which was often printed on his tournament shirt, is "If I can, you can."

One of my bucket-list items is to fish with Clay. His angling skills, personality, and positive attitude make me want to be around him. Clay is simply different from other people, and it's the ways that he's unique that make him intriguing.

There's a push these days to try to present Christianity as if it's a normal, *not-weird* faith system. We speak to others about Jesus as if He's not radical or unique from other mainstream leaders. But that's simply not the case. Jesus was different from any other person who walked the earth. His message of the kingdom of God seemed foolish to those who didn't believe, as Paul describes in 1 Corinthians 1:18: "For the word of the cross is folly to those who are perishing, but to us who are being saved it is the power of God."

The uniqueness of Christ hasn't changed in two thousand years. When rightly described, the biblical narrative still strikes the ears as odd. Think of the story: it starts with a naked married couple in a garden; this couple eventually disobeys their Creator by believing lies that a snake tells them; and God banishes them from the garden, but only after killing an animal to clothe their nakedness and shame.

Hang with me, because it gets even stranger. The Gospels tell us that several centuries later, the same God who banished Adam and Eve from the garden became a human being. He was homeless. He walked on water. He spent time with the disabled, sick, and poor. In John 6,

He deeply offended the (kosher) religious leaders by telling them, "Whoever feeds on my flesh and drinks my blood has eternal life, and I will raise him up on the last day. For my flesh is true food, and my blood is true drink. Whoever feeds on my flesh and drinks my blood abides in me, and I in him" (vv. 54–56).

It gets odder still! Toward the end of the Gospels, we learn that the same God who killed an animal to cover the shame of Adam and Eve gave up His own life on the cross to cover our shame for all eternity. He was buried in a tomb, but He rose from the dead three days later, appearing to hundreds of His followers. What did He say to them? He told them to go into every place in the world and make disciples. And, oh yeah, He commanded that all the new disciples be publicly dunked into water to symbolize their new life in Jesus. Then we read that Jesus floated up into heaven before sending the Spirit of God to them "like a mighty rushing wind" (Acts 2:2b).

How is Jesus not the strangest, most intriguing person you've ever encountered?

How is the gospel story, start to finish, not the wildest tale you've ever heard?

For the past two thousand years, many have rejected Jesus as a liar or a lunatic, to borrow C. S. Lewis's labels. For many, Jesus and the gospel were too strange to believe. But for a few, Jesus and the gospel were too strange *not* to believe. These people looked at Jesus' words and deeds and saw the Lord. They saw Jesus' uniqueness and were drawn to Him because of it.

Clay Dyer is in that group. There's another way Clay stands out in this world: he believes in Jesus and shares the gospel every chance he gets. I heard Clay give his testimony once. He described how a friend invited him to a youth rally. Before the event, Clay felt anxiety coursing through his body. It was such a forceful feeling he thought he might be dying. It scared him. It also opened his eyes to believe that the strange claims of the gospel are true. When the pastor talked about the finished work of Jesus, Clay got up, slid out of the pew, and moved toward the front. He prayed the salvation prayer and was immediately flooded with the peace of Jesus, his Savior.

We'd have to change the biblical story to present Christianity as a mainstream option. For us to present Jesus as "a regular guy who won't shock you at all," we'd have to change the biblical facts about Him. We must let Jesus be Jesus. We must present Him in precisely the manner He appears in the Bible. Those people we're praying for, the ones we hope will find salvation in Christ, need to see how our Savior is unlike anyone they've ever met before.

QUESTIONS FOR FURTHER REFLECTION:

1. Do you feel the desire to present Christianity as a perfectly rational option? If so, what's behind this motivation?
2. Are you living out the gospel with such truthfulness that you likely appear odd and intriguing to a world that needs to see your odd and intriguing Messiah? If so, how could you do that even more?
3. Can you remember the first time you heard about Jesus? In what ways did the gospel story seem strange?

16

ANGLERS, REALLY?

And it is yet more observable, that when our blessed Saviour went up into the mount, when he left the rest of his disciples, and chose only three to bear him company at his Transfiguration, that those three were all fishermen.

Izaak Walton, *The Compleat Angler*

Scripture to Read: Psalm 34:4–5; Matthew 4:17–25

The first four people Jesus called to follow Him were fishermen. While sitting in the cab of my truck, sopping wet from head to toe, face red from embarrassment, I questioned Jesus' choice.

I blame the entire debacle on a pair of sunglasses. Last spring, right before a trip to Montana, I ordered a pair of polarized shades. I purchased the brand I trust, but this pair had a feature I'd never tried: magnifiers built into the bottom third of the lens. They were perfect for threading tiny tippet through minute eyelets while standing in a river.

They were not so perfect, it turns out, for seeing the boulders in the river my boots were about to trip on as I moved from spot to spot. Looking down at my feet was like looking out a windshield with broken wipers in a downpour.

The Missouri River was packed with anglers that morning, which meant that I entertained a great crowd for hours. If I wasn't tumbling headfirst into the ice-cold water, I was stepping into a hole and disappearing before their eyes. What's more, I discovered that it's impossible to establish a rhythm in your cast and delicacy in your presentation when dozens of people up and down the river have ceased their own fishing to see what mistake you'll make next. Not only did I stumble around like a drunken sailor, but I also tangled my line and hooked tree branches one after another.

Jesus wants us to source our identity and confidence from Him. He wants us to find our significance, worth, and purpose in what He did for us, not in what we accomplish or how well we perform.

Over the lunch hour, having left all my dignity in the river, I returned to my truck and hung my waders upside down on the tailgate to empty and dry. I hopped into the sun-warmed cab to read the day's entry in a devotional. The book had me read Matthew 4, which recounts the moment when Jesus called Simon, Andrew, James, and John—*four fishermen*—to be His first students. As the smell of wet wool wafted up from my socks and filled the cab with an aromatic reminder of my clumsiness, I wondered why Jesus would choose fishermen as His first representatives.

We must wait until we meet our Savior face-to-face for the complete answer. However, the Scriptures tell us that Jesus came to seek and save ordinary people, not merely the world's gifted, well-educated, surefooted anglers.

In first-century Jewish culture, most little boys and girls studied the Torah, the first five books of the Hebrew Scriptures. At around age ten, the boys began apprenticing under their father to learn his trade. The girls started working alongside their older sisters and their mother.

The exception was if a boy demonstrated remarkable abilities to memorize and understand the Torah. Such a boy would be sent to school for another five years to memorize the rest of the Hebrew Scriptures. At fourteen or fifteen, most of these boys would return home to work with their fathers, but the truly exceptional students would seek a rabbi to follow. The most revered rabbis in Israel were highly selective about who could follow them. To maintain their reputations, they invited only the best of the best.

Because they were fishermen by trade (and not students of other rabbis), we can be sure that Simon, Andrew, James, and John weren't the best of the best. When Jesus called fishermen to be His first ambassadors, He made a poignant statement: He wasn't looking for elites, seeking the most talented or the most educated. He wasn't recruiting the fishermen who moved with grace and cast with perfect rhythm. Jesus was starting a movement, one that continues today, of inviting ordinary people with wet socks and empty fly boxes to follow Him.

This world values high performance. It gives extra honor to the wealthy, beautiful, and talented. It especially esteems superstar athletes and celebrities, people who use their talents to entertain us. We pay professional athletes fifteen thousand times what we pay teachers.

(I know this because a dear friend of mine signed a teaching contract for forty-six thousand dollars a year in the same week that Shohei Ohtani signed a ten-year contract with the Dodgers for seven hundred million.)

This world wants superstar entertainers.

Jesus wants *you*.

His movement is not of this world. It doesn't follow the human performance patterns we're used to. In Luke 10, when Jesus sent out seventy-two people to preach about the kingdom of God, they were brand-new believers. They barely knew anything about Jesus. What's more, they were ordinary, common villagers. They carried little privilege or respect in society. We see this in how they returned excited because "even the demons are subject to us in your name!" (v. 17b). These people weren't used to getting a response like that. Before their mission for Jesus, nobody took them seriously. Now, as Jesus' representatives, even demons took them seriously.

Jesus tells them not to make too much of that, for that would be to fall back into the world's performance patterns. He says to them, "Nevertheless, do not rejoice in this, that the spirits are subject to you, but rejoice that your names are written in heaven" (v. 20).

Jesus doesn't want us to find our identity and confidence in our ministry's success. He wants us to source our identity and confidence from Him. He wants us to find our significance, worth, and purpose in what He did for us, not in what we accomplish or how well we perform.

Do you have clumsy days on the water, in the home, or on the job? Do you feel ordinary? Or, at times, far worse, like I felt that morning in Montana when I spent more time under the water than above it? It's okay. You are anything but ordinary if you've taken Jesus up on

His invitation to follow Him. You belong to Jesus now. You have His power and wisdom at work in your life.

What's more, some of the ways you are ordinary, average, or even flat-out clumsy are precisely the areas in your life that will preach the gospel the loudest. Paul writes:

> He said to me, "My grace is sufficient for you, for my power is made perfect in weakness." Therefore I will boast all the more gladly of my weaknesses, so that the power of Christ may rest upon me. For the sake of Christ, then, I am content with weaknesses, insults, hardships, persecutions, and calamities. For when I am weak, then I am strong. (2 Cor. 12:9–10)

QUESTIONS FOR FURTHER REFLECTION:

1. In what ways do you feel average or perhaps flat-out clumsy? Have you ever considered that those parts of you might be the ones that share the message of Christ the clearest?
2. Do you feel tempted to find your significance, worth, and purpose in your accomplishments? Do you catch yourself when you do this?
3. How could seeing yourself as Jesus' disciple change how you go about your typical day?

17

LOOK AGAIN

So forth and brighter fares my stream,—
Who drink it shall not thirst again;
No darkness taints its equal gleam,
And ages drop in it like rain.

Ralph Waldo Emerson, "Two Rivers"

Scripture to Read: John 20:19–29; Revelation 5:1–14

In the early 2000s, a poor fisherman from the Philippines was out to sea when a fierce storm developed. The waves were breaking on the barrier reef with such force that the fisherman anchored his boat and spent the night at sea.

The following day, when he tried to hoist the anchor, it wouldn't budge. Thinking it was hooked on a rock or coral reef, he dove into the ocean to free the anchor. To his surprise, it was snagged on a monstrous clam. The fisherman managed to get the clam into the boat. That was when he noticed a large shiny object nestled inside the shell. He pulled it out, but not knowing what it was, he took it home, put it in a bag, and hid it under his bed.

The Filipino fisherman continued to fish for the next ten years. He struggled to make ends meet. He eventually decided to move into a different home. "He'd almost forgotten everything about" it, but then "he remembered he had something under his bed," Aileen Cynthia Maggay-Amurao told a CNN reporter.[14]

Maggay-Amurao was Puerto Princesa's tourism officer, and she put out an online request asking for gemologists to help identify the object. She discovered that what the fisherman hid under his bed was likely the largest pearl ever found, measuring more than two feet long and weighing seventy-five pounds. The fisherman requested to remain anonymous. The pearl, however, was named—the Pearl of Puerto Princesa—and was estimated to be worth one hundred million dollars.

This story reminds us that sometimes our first assumptions couldn't be more wrong. This was perhaps most forcefully demonstrated when Jesus was on the cross. When Jesus' nearly naked body hung on the cross, both the Romans and the Israelites scorned Him. As His blood ran down His legs and pooled on the stones below, they saw Him as a fool. They mocked Him and hurled insults at Him. At that moment, Jesus appeared defeated.

Even the disciples despaired. They'd spent three years listening to Jesus talk of the kingdom of heaven, and now the One they believed was the long-awaited King hung dying on a tree. According to the Scriptures, to die on a cross proved that God had cursed that man. Deuteronomy 21:22–23a records, "If a man has committed a crime punishable by death and he is put to death, and you hang him on a tree, his body shall not remain all night on the tree, but you shall bury him the same day, for a hanged man is cursed by God."

To those present, the cross displayed Jesus' shame and defeat. But their first impressions couldn't have been more wrong. The cross of Christ is the moment in the Gospels when the power and glory of God are most displayed. The onlookers missed this—for the same reason that many of us fail to see it today. We think glory is proved by powerful titles, great wealth, and the ability to make others do what we want. Our categories are simple and formulaic. If we experience shame, we think we lack glory. If we die, we think we aren't victorious.

But the kingdom of God is not like the kingdom of this world. Jesus' crucifixion, while being the moment He bore our shame and died for our sins, was also the moment that the power of God crushed His enemies: our sins and the spiritual forces of darkness.

This is why Jesus' resurrected body still has the scars of the cross on His hands and feet. This is why John, in his vision of the throne room of God, describes "a Lamb standing, as though it had been slain" (Rev. 5:6b). We think of scars, especially ones created by moments of defeat, as proof of loss. We cover them up. We hide them because we hate retelling embarrassing stories. Yet Jesus' resurrected body bears the scars of the cross. Why?

It's because the scars of His humiliation and death are the evidence of His victory over sin and death. His scars of shame are His marks of glory, as John records in Revelation 5:9b–10:

> *Worthy are you* to take the scroll
> and to open its seals,
> *for you were slain*, and by your blood you ransomed
> people for God
> from every tribe and language and people and nation,
> and you have made them a kingdom and priests to
> our God,
> and they shall reign on the earth.

The next time we remember our Savior's cross through the ordinance of the Lord's Supper, may we consider both His shame and His glory. His death and His victory over death. His crown of thorns and His crown as the King of Kings.

QUESTIONS FOR FURTHER REFLECTION:

1. How does the fact that Jesus' glory and power were most displayed at the cross change how you think about glory and power? In what ways does this truth challenge your aspirations for glory and power?
2. What does it look like for us to follow Jesus by denying ourselves and taking up our cross, as He described in Matthew 16:24–25: "Then Jesus told his disciples, 'If anyone would come after me, let him deny himself and take up his cross and follow me. For whoever would save his life will lose it, but whoever loses his life for my sake will find it'"?
3. What is a specific step you can take this week to strive for greatness according to God's definition—"For he who is least among you all is the one who is great" (Luke 9:48b)?

18

AVERAGE AT EVERYTHING

It has always been my private conviction that any man who pits his intelligence against a fish and loses has it coming.

John Steinbeck, "On Fishing"

Scripture to Read: Matthew 11:25–29; 2 Corinthians 5:16–21

I'm an average fisherman. I was forced to that conclusion after a couple of days of fishing in Missouri several years ago. The trip combined my two favorite types of angling—slinging Texas rigs and spinners for bass and fly fishing for trout. On the first day, my cousin zipped me around Table Rock Lake on his tournament bass boat. I learned that sixty-five miles an hour on a boat feels faster than a hundred miles an hour on a motorcycle—and that you'd better keep your mouth shut or you'll be picking bugs out of your teeth.

Watching my cousin fish was like watching a conductor lead an orchestra. Every cast presented the lure precisely where he intended. He had multiple rigs set up and stored neatly within reach to maximize the casts he'd get that day. I, on the other hand, had two rods and reels, both coated with road-gravel dust from being stored in our garage. We both caught fish that day, but I purposely didn't write down the final numbers. My cousin managed the boat, putting me in all the best spots, but he outfished me by a mile.

Having fished with my cousin that day, I met my friend Steve the next day at Roaring River State Park. Steve is a true trout bum; he guides anglers on several rivers and then fishes them for himself on his days off. Fishing with Steve is like sitting in class, only instead of blackboards and chalk, the river and his fly box are his tools of instruction. Not that Steve sees himself as a teacher. It's just that when you watch someone present a dry fly on the surface of the water an inch above a trout's nose, with no pull or drag on the surface, you can't help but take notes.

I was new to fly fishing and, all day long, my imitation mayfly slapped the water or landed on top of a bundle of tippet. Steve's fly stopped in midair just above the water, then fell to the surface even better than the real blue-winged olives were doing it.

Back when I was in my teens and twenties, I never would have admitted to being average. Even if I knew that someone was better than I was, I'd keep my mouth shut, work harder, and make it my goal to prove myself the next time. As I write this devotion, I'm now in my early fifties, and it doesn't bother me to put in ink that I'm average at most things. In fact, these days, I prefer to fish with people who are better than I am. I enjoy celebrating their skills and learning new techniques from them.

What has changed throughout the past twenty years? What's made me comfortable in my own skin, even if my skin is wrinkled and flawed?

I've come to believe that my accomplishments do not define me. I've come to trust that those who are "in Christ" always measure up to God's standards, no matter how well they're performing, because of the righteousness of His Son. To have Christ is to have the infinite worthiness of Jesus, the perfection of His life, and the completed work of His cross. For Christians, Jesus is now our life. *He* is our standing before God. He is our performance. He is our accomplishment. His life, death, and resurrection have eternally settled the question of our significance.

This is called our *union with Christ*, and it's the most life-changing truth I've encountered. Herman Bavinck writes,

> The combination *in Christ* (in the Lord, in Him) occurs more than a hundred and fifty times in the New Testament. It indicates that Christ is the constant source not only of the spiritual life, but that as such He also immediately and directly dwells in the believer. The unity is as close as that between a cornerstone and a temple, a man and a woman, the head and the body, the vine and the branch.[15]

As the mighty Arkansas River weaves through Missouri, so the doctrine of our union with Christ flows throughout the New Testament. The Lord used Paul's letters to the Corinthians to open my eyes and free me from a life of performance. In 2005, I studied and preached 1 and 2 Corinthians verse by verse. The Christians in Corinth had the same problems I struggled with: they tried to find their worth in performing better than others.

- "I'm better than you because I follow the right celebrities."

- "I'm a cut above you because I make more money."
- "I'm superior because I have a better title or role in society."

In 1 Corinthians 11, we learn that even the Lord's Supper was used to divide people by social class and income.

Throughout his letters, Paul urged the Christians in Corinth to stop basing their identity on their accomplishments, income, and titles. He reminds them that their identity is now based on Christ alone. Paul writes in 2 Corinthians 5:21, "For our sake he made him to be sin who knew no sin, so that in him we might become the righteousness of God."

To have Christ is to have the infinite worthiness of Jesus, the perfection of His life, and the completed work of His cross.... He is our standing before God. He is our performance. He is our accomplishment. His life, death, and resurrection have eternally settled the question of our significance.

Many Christians are exhausted and weary. They say they are grateful for their salvation, but they still feel a constant pressure to prove themselves by what they do. To these Christians, the easy yoke and light burden Jesus spoke of make no sense whatsoever (Matt. 11: 28–30).

This is how I felt as I began studying Paul's letters. Through the Word, the Spirit showed me that I wasn't allowing the doctrine of my union with Christ to work deep into my soul, into the very fiber of my being, to free me from my desires to prove myself. My prayer during that season was, "God, help me so clearly understand and believe who I am in Christ that I might finally find the easy yoke and light burden Jesus offers. Help me enjoy my identity in Christ during both my high-achieving and low-achieving moments."

My fellow angler, if your soul is weary from trying to prove yourself by your actions, let me invite you to pray that same prayer. Take it from one unexceptionally average angler to someone who is likely another: God loves that prayer. He will answer it. You will find rest for your soul.

QUESTIONS FOR FURTHER REFLECTION:

1. What accomplishments or achievements do you feel tempted to use as proof that you measure up (e.g., athletics, income, title, or ministry position)?
2. Have you had a hard time understanding or experiencing the easy yoke and light burden Jesus offers? Do you know anyone who seems to enjoy Jesus' yoke? If so, consider asking them to pray for you and share their counsel from the Scriptures.
3. According to the Scriptures (see Rom. 6:5; 2 Cor. 5:17; Eph. 1:3–4), how does being united with Christ change the way God views you? How does being united with Christ change the way you view yourself?

19

SHORELINE MEALS

O flames that glowed! O hearts that yearned!
They were indeed too much akin,
The drift-wood fire without that burned,
The thoughts that burned and glowed within.

Henry Wadsworth Longfellow, "The Fire of Drift-Wood"

Scripture to Read: Luke 24:1–43

I doubled my tip because of the shoreline lunch. One of the first times I fly fished in Montana, I hired a guide, Trent, to take me to the Gallatin River. When we met at Trent's shop at daybreak, he asked me if I'd like sandwiches for lunch or if I'd "be up for something adventurous." I'll always take the *adventurous* option, food-wise. Choosing it that day proved to be one of the best culinary decisions of my life.

Around one o'clock, I hooked an eighteen-inch rainbow. Trent measured the fish with a ruler on his landing net. "Perfect timing and perfect-sized fish for lunch! I'll get started," he said. "You keep casting."

I positioned myself a few feet from the bank so I could watch Trent work. He gathered some twisted, dry driftwood and lit a fire on the pebbled beach near the water. While the flames crackled and popped, Trent cleaned the fish in the river beside me. When the driftwood burned down into red-hot embers, he placed a large cast-iron pan on the coals. That's when the magic happened.

Trent put a generous pad of butter in the skillet. As it sizzled, he rotated the pan so the creamy golden deliciousness spread evenly over the face.

Trent wet the fish in the river then dropped it into a mixture of flour, salt, pepper, and Parmesan cheese. He placed the fish on the butter on one side of the pan. On the other side, he put a handful of fresh asparagus and two homemade buttermilk biscuits. He flipped the fish in the pan and stirred the asparagus. He cooked them perfectly, beautifully searing everything in the pan.

When the dish was ready, Trent used a fork to remove the meat from one side of the trout, and he piled it on his plate. He placed the rest of the fish on my plate. When he served the asparagus and biscuits, he pulled a Tupperware container from the cooler and asked if I'd like to try his homemade tartar sauce. I nodded enthusiastically. He drizzled the creamy topping onto the trout and asparagus.

We sat on the bank and feasted. I ate as slowly as possible, taking small bites and pausing frequently to admire the meal and praise the friend who had prepared it.

That was the most surprising fish meal I've ever had. However, it isn't the most shocking one this world has ever known. That one, I'd argue, is recorded in Luke 24.

The moment takes place after Jesus rose from the dead. He had appeared to the two disciples on the road to Emmaus, and they had just run all the way back to Jerusalem to tell the other disciples, who were locked in the upper room. Luke records, "As they were talking about these things, Jesus himself stood among them, and said to them, 'Peace to you!'" (Luke 24:36).

Jesus greeted them with "Peace to you," but the disciples felt anything but peaceful. They were shocked and afraid. Perhaps they thought Jesus was some kind of spook or spirit. Jesus displayed His wounded hands and feet to them as proof that it really was Him. The Eleven saw His scars, but it still seemed too good to be true.

That's when Jesus did something so ordinary that it was shocking: He asked them for food. Luke writes, "While they still disbelieved for joy and were marveling, he said to them, 'Have you anything here to eat?' They gave him a piece of broiled fish, and he took it and ate before them" (Luke 24:41–43).

Why is this detail in this resurrection account?

The simplest answer is: because it happened. Luke, the fastidious doctor-turned-gospel-writer, cared deeply about the facts. The details mattered, so much so that Luke included the specific method the disciples had used to prepare the fish—they had broiled it.

This detail is also included in the account for our encouragement. Luke wanted us to be amazed by the same truth that astonished the eleven disciples: the One who was crucified came back. He rose from the dead in His physical body, a body that could be recognized by His friends. A body with wounds they'd seen Him receive. And a body that wanted to eat fish.

Consider two other astonishing implications of Jesus' bodily resurrection: first, it reminds us that our bodies are gifts from God and are inherently valuable. This was not a common thought in Jesus' day. In the first century, most people believed that the material world was corrupt and that if they really wanted to be with God, they had to escape their physical bodies.

When Jesus rose from the dead, He proved He was God. And when He rose from the dead in His physical body, He proved that there isn't a sacred-secular divide between the immaterial and the material world. God's perfect design for humanity includes a mysteriously beautiful body-soul connection.

The bodily resurrection of Jesus also shows us that we have an eternity of physical enjoyment and pleasures forevermore ahead of us. There's something in our hearts that wants the good times in this life to never end—moments like I had with Trent on the Gallatin. For those who are in Christ, the good times don't end. Death can't stop them. If the grave couldn't keep Jesus from enjoying broiled fish with His friends, it can't keep us from delicious feasts with Him either. This is our great hope as Christians: thanks to Jesus, the best is yet to come.

QUESTIONS FOR FURTHER REFLECTION:

1. During the Last Supper, Jesus told His disciples, "I tell you I will not drink again of this fruit of the vine until that day when I drink it new with you in my Father's kingdom" (Matt. 26:29). What do you imagine feasting with Jesus at His table will be like?
2. Do you tend to downgrade the importance of your body (body shaming) or treat it as if it is more important than it was meant to be (body worship)? When you consider your body as a gift from God

so you can enjoy life with Him and others, what does it look like to honor that gift appropriately?

3. What are some of the physical enjoyments and pleasures forevermore that you look forward to when you consider eternity with God in your resurrected body?

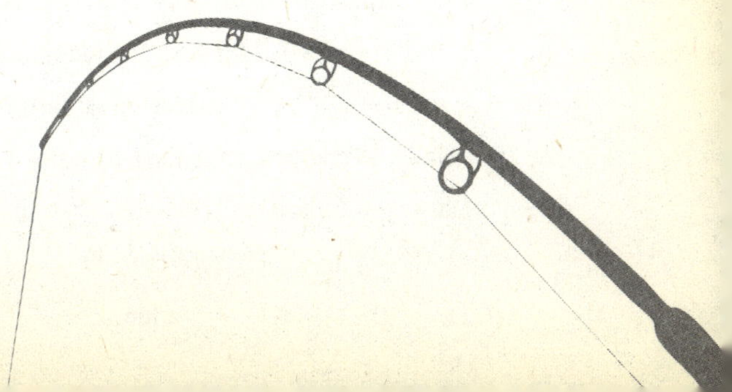

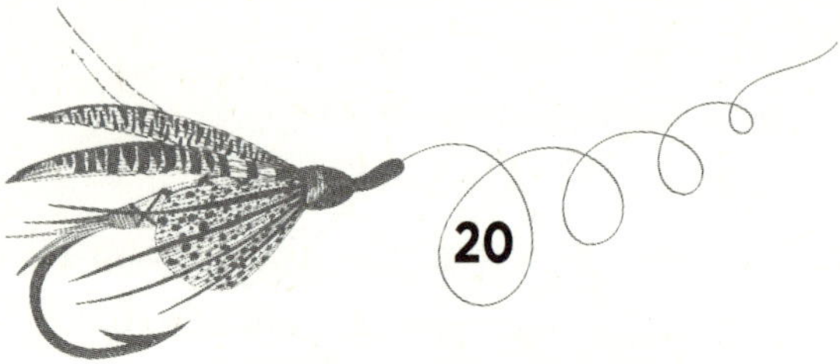

20

TOGETHER

She was charmed by the motions of the trout. How they take their forms from the pressures of another world, the cold forge of water. Their drift, their mystery, the way they turn and let the current take them, take them, with passive grace.

Matthew Neill Null, *Allegheny Front*

Scripture to Read: John 16:5–15; Ephesians 3:14–19

My son, Aidan, is my river buddy. I took all three of our children fishing when they were young, but he's the one who adopted my passion for the sport. Throughout his high school years, we fished farm ponds and sandpit lakes near our house, and the summer after he graduated, we fished several of Montana's and Wyoming's best waters. Before the trip, I made him a landing net out of catalpa and walnut from trees that had stood tried and true along the river near our property.

A couple of months later, Aidan loaded up his Subaru and headed west to attend college in Denver. The busyness of studies, sports, and work kept us from entering a river or stream together for more than a year and a half. We kept each other present during our times outside. When he and his friend Elijah fished the South Platte in Colorado, they texted photos of black spots on pink-and-green rainbows in Aidan's landing net. I'd call him with the report when I fished Long Pine Creek in northern Nebraska. These updates were bittersweet; they helped us feel connected while reminding us we were apart.

How our children leave home and move away strikes me as wrong, almost unnatural. Parents work hard to teach and guide their children to become the kind of adults they enjoy being around. Then, when children become such adults, they leave. Of course, college and work are essential; we saved money to help Aidan and his sisters leave home to continue their growth and education. I'm simply inviting any parent reading this book to join me in mourning the loss of being near the kids we love.

God gives us this longing to enjoy our children's company. It's His heart, and He shared it with us. From the beginning, our heavenly Father has wanted to be with us. He didn't create Eden and then step back—He made it and *entered* it. In Genesis 3:8, we read about how the Lord walked in the garden in the cool of the day. This description shows up after Adam and Eve sinned. We don't know for sure, but I don't think this was the first time God had walked with Adam and Eve. But it *was* the first time Adam and Eve had been afraid of God. Sin makes us want to hide from the One who wants to be with us.

Even Adam and Eve's sins didn't dissuade God from being near His people. God walked with the Israelites as they journeyed away from Egypt and toward the Promised Land, His presence represented by pillars of clouds and fire.

The New Testament opens with God entering His creation to walk with us again, yet in a shockingly new way: He took the form of a baby with chubby little legs, legs that would one day have the strength to walk with friends from town to town. The incarnation screams to the world that our God loves being with us.

So does the giving of the Holy Spirit. Jesus told His disciples that Him leaving them to return to His Father was to their benefit. In John 16:7, Jesus says, "Nevertheless, I tell you the truth: it is to your advantage that I go away, for if I do not go away, the Helper will not come to you. But if I go, I will send him to you."

The incarnation screams to the world that our God loves being with us.

Later, when Jesus rose from the dead and appeared to a large group of His followers, telling them of His need to ascend to His Father, He again promised to clothe them with power (i.e., to send the Helper to them; see Acts 1:8). Think of what an emotionally challenging idea that would have been to Jesus' community. They loved Jesus as I love Aidan. Jesus was their rabbi, son, brother, and friend. His friends and family knew His voice, expressions, and mannerisms. They enjoyed hugging Him and listening to Him laugh. As nothing in their hearts had wanted Him to die, now that they had Him back, no part of them wanted Him to leave.

Yet Jesus knew that when He left, the Father would send the Spirit. The coming of the Spirit would be to their "advantage" because He would give them, and us today, an even more personal experience of God's presence.

In Ephesians 3:16–17a, Paul prays for the church "that according to the riches of [God's] glory he may grant you to be strengthened with power through his Spirit in your inner being, so that Christ may dwell in your hearts through faith."

Note that the Ephesians he was writing to were already Christians. This isn't a prayer for their salvation, nor is it a prayer that they would have more of Christ or more of the Holy Spirit. To be a Christian is to have all of Christ and to be wholly baptized by the Spirit. Paul is praying for an even sweeter, richer communion with God—"that Christ may dwell in your hearts through faith."

This is why it's not accurate to see Christianity as a religion or a checklist of rights and wrongs. God created us to be with Him. Jesus, our Savior, made that possible by His life, death, and resurrection. Thanks to Jesus, we are united to Christ and in union with our triune God. We are once again with God, and God is with us.

The Holy Spirit, the third person in the Trinity, gives us that sweet communion with God. The Spirit convicts us of our sins. He opens our eyes to the truth of the gospel. He illuminates God's Word for us. He applies the grace and mercy of God to us. He bears fruit in us and through us. He strengthens our inner being so we may know God is with us. Michael Reeves writes, "[The Spirit] enlightens us to know the love of God, and that light warms us, drawing us to love him and to overflow with love to others."[16]

Let us praise the Spirit of God, the One who removes our desire to hide from the Lord. Thanks to Him, God's footsteps are no longer a fearful sound.

The summer after Aidan's sophomore year, we fished together once again. On a drive to the North Platte River in Wyoming with friends, I called Aidan to see if he could join us. He and Elijah drove up that evening. The following day, we tucked into our favorite spot on the river and fished for eight hours. Toward the end of the afternoon, a blue-winged olive hatch brought the trout to the surface. The water looked like it was boiling. I stood beside Aidan as he hooked, fought, and netted several fish on a dry fly.

There were plenty of fish to catch. I could have walked a short distance up or down the river to cast my line as well.

I didn't want to. Even a short distance from my son in those final minutes of the day would've been too far.

QUESTIONS FOR FURTHER REFLECTION:

1. Do you sense the Spirit of God giving you the experience of fellowship with our triune God each day? Explain your answer.
2. Jesus describes the Spirit as a "Helper" in John 14:16. Describe a time when the Spirit of God comforted you when you were depressed or anxious.
3. Is it hard to picture God next to you delighting in being with you the way I delighted in being near Aidan? If so, I encourage you to read the three parables in Luke 15. Before you read, pray and ask God to show you how precious you are to Him.

21

SALT

The rule here, as it is in Montana, is that you can fish through any private property as long as you stay in the streambed.

John Gierach, *Dumb Luck and the Kindness of Strangers*

Scripture to Read: Matthew 5:13–16; 1 Peter 3:13–17

It's hard to relax when a plane is circling you. I was alone, standing in a small stream near the abandoned town of Lombard, Montana, and a plane was buzzing me.

Lombard sprang up in 1895 at the junction of two railroads, the Northern Pacific and the Milwaukee Road. The town had a post office, a school, and the High Point Inn. The village had rested in a narrow valley at the base of several mountains along the Missouri River. In 1930, the state put in a road over one of the steep peaks, but the town remained accessed primarily by trains. The population slowly declined. By the time the Milwaukee Road railroad closed in 1980, it was officially a ghost town.

I was renting a cabin from a family who lived across the river from the ghost town. When I arrived, I asked the owner for suggestions on where to fish. I knew of Montana's big rivers but was eager to find smaller, less-populated waters. He pointed across the Missouri and said, "It's hard to get to, but Sixteen Mile Creek is over there. It's loaded with trout."

He described how the old 1930 road was still somewhat accessible. He explained that, once I drove over the hill and through the remains of Lombard, I could park next to an old bridge over Sixteen Mile Creek and slip down the bank into the water. All the land in that area was private property. However, Montana's laws allow anglers to access and fish rivers and streams if they enter on public land and stay within the river's high-water mark.

I followed my friend's directions, entering the river at the bridge. I fished my way downstream, catching a good number of brook trout.

A couple of hours later, I heard an airplane. In the distance, I saw a small plane, not much bigger than a compact car, flying toward me. When it cleared the mountains, it dropped to about seventy feet above me and circled continuously for the next twenty minutes. The plane was so close that I could see the eyes of its sole occupant, eyes that were fixed on me almost the entire time.

I tried to dismiss his presence, but pretending a plane isn't circling you is like trying to forget you have a toothache. He was there, and he was staying there until he drove me from the river. His plan worked. I walked upstream and exited the water at the bridge. That's when the aircraft straightened its wings and flew back toward where it'd come.

The pilot pressured me with his presence to get what he wanted: me gone. In a similar manner, some Christians try to advance Christ's kingdom by fighting and arguing in the same ways the world fights and argues. Like that pilot in the peaceful valley, many Christians enter public spaces shaming and belittling those who disagree with their faith and political positions. Sometimes, they direct their attack toward non-Christians, sometimes toward those within the camp.

As salt is scattered on a tasty dish, God has scattered us, His church, across the world to keep the flavors and aromas of the kingdom of God always before those who need Christ.

Perhaps this stems from a misunderstanding of salt and saltiness. A while back, I spoke with a popular Christian figure, someone known for quick words and sharp put-downs. When I asked where he got the vision for that type of debate, he replied, "Jesus called us to be the salt of the world." He added, "Salt's not fun. Just put a spoonful in your mouth and see how it tastes."

This Christian leader seemed to adhere to the world's definition of salty. Salty is slang today for someone who is bitter and angry and carries a chip on their shoulder. If someone responds defensively and escalates the situation, they're likely to hear, "Why so salty?"

But is this the saltiness Jesus is calling us to when He tells us we are the salt of the earth? Examining how salt was used in the first century helps us answer this question. Salt was essential for flavoring and preserving food. This appears to be the heart of Jesus' metaphor when we consider His warning: "But if salt has lost its taste, how shall its saltiness be restored? It is no longer good for anything except to be thrown out and trampled under people's feet" (Matt. 5:13b).

The flavoring power of salt represents enjoyment and the pleasures of feasting. The preserving nature of salt symbolizes future nourishment and food security. One of my favorite chefs, Michael Ruhlman, writes, "[Salt] allowed food to travel long distances, either as goods to trade or as sustenance for long voyages in world exploration. Salt was once more valuable than precious metals; men were paid with it."[17]

How are we to be the "salt of the earth," then? By living as witnesses to Christ in such a way that we show the precious, preserving nature of the kingdom of God. When the gospel is lived out and presented by (the right kind of) salty Christians, it offers the joy of the Lord to the world. It offers a secure future filled with nourishment and provision for all our souls' needs. As the psalmist declares, "In your presence there is fullness of joy; at your right hand are pleasures forevermore" (Ps. 16:11b).

In his commentary on Matthew, Rudolf Schnackenburg writes, "Together with the image of the lamp, it [salt] is an appeal to the community of disciples to bear witness to the gospel, in the midst of a world still averse to it, by living a life in conformity with Jesus' instructions."[18]

As salt is scattered on a tasty dish, God has scattered us, His church, across the world to keep the flavors and aromas of the kingdom of God always before those who need Christ. We preach the gospel. We persuade. We urge. We witness. We speak the truth.

But we do not manipulate, coerce, shame, pressure, belittle, dehumanize, or intimidate. Those weren't Jesus' ways, and they shouldn't be ours. The salty qualities of the kingdom of God, delivered through the witness of Christians, must penetrate the hearts of lost people so they may be saved. The heart is where the kingdom of God resides. The heart is what matters. The world's ways offend hearts. Christ's ways win them.

My friend, let us not be like the pilot who drove me from the water. Rather, let us be salty witnesses of the risen Christ who invite people to the life-giving waters we've found.

QUESTIONS FOR FURTHER REFLECTION:

1. What are ways that you are being a salty Christian, someone who keeps the flavor and aroma of the kingdom of God present in the life of your community?
2. Can you remember a time when you tried to pressure or argue someone into believing in the gospel? If so, how did they respond?
3. In what ways does the following verse challenge your current approach to being salt and light: "In your hearts honor Christ the Lord as holy, always being prepared to make a defense to anyone who asks you for a reason for the hope that is in you; yet do it with gentleness and respect" (1 Pet. 3:15)?

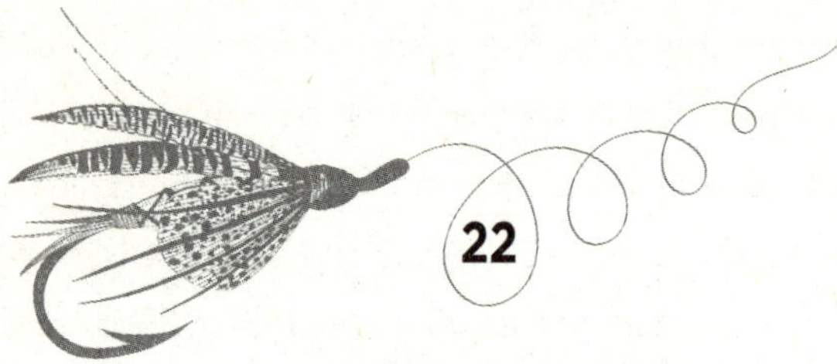

22

ONE AIM

You are no failure, on a river. The water moves regardless—
for all it cares, you might be a minnow or a tadpole, a
turtle on a beavered log. You might be nothing at all.

Leif Enger, *So Brave, Young, and Handsome*

Scripture to Read: Jeremiah 9:23–24; John 3:25–36

On April 15, 1984, William Garvey shattered the Arkansas white bass state record. The previous record fish, taken from Beaver Lake, had been four pounds fifteen ounces. Garvey's lunker beat it by a solid three ounces. The previous record had stood for almost fifteen years, so it seemed likely that Garvey's impressive fish would remain at the top for quite some time.

"Quite some time" proved to be later that same day. Just a few hours later, William Wilson, Garvey's fishing buddy, throwing a deep-running Rebel crankbait, hooked and landed a white bass that weighed five pounds four ounces.[19]

Garvey and Wilson were both from Indiana, but they'd clearly figured out Arkansas. Barry McKenzie, the Arkansas Game and Fish Commission wildlife officer who verified the weights of both fish, told a reporter, "In addition to two record fish, they had several that weighed more than 4 pounds."[20]

When I read about William Garvey's short-lived record, it reminded me of one of my own. When I was a young man, I wanted to break records. I was a competitive swimmer throughout junior high and high school. When I entered my senior year, I wanted to win the state championship and see my name on the trophy. That year, I swam the backstroke leg on our medley relay at the state meet. We had a fast squad. We won state and broke the record by almost a second. A second is a considerable margin in a two-hundred-yard event. We were confident that our time would stand at the top for years to come.

It lasted twelve months. My alma mater's relay squad beat it by half a second the following year, replacing our names in Nebraska's record books.

At the time, I felt sad about losing the record. Looking back, I'm incredibly grateful for its short life. In fact, when I consider all my short-lived victories and numerous defeats, I'm thankful for all of them. The fleeting nature of victory and the lasting stings of defeat showed me how small my life was when my aim was to make a name for myself. For the first twenty years of my life, I was the living, breathing, swimming example of Philippians 2:21, which says, "For they all seek their own interests, not those of Jesus Christ."

When I became a Christian, in college, the Scriptures presented me with a different way to live. I discovered the vision in John's gospel.

In John 1, John the Baptist announced the coming of the Messiah. John was gaining popularity, and a large crowd of people were venturing into the wilderness to hear him preach. This world loves its celebrities, and John's crowd wanted to turn him into the one they followed. But John redirected their hopes to the coming Christ, saying, "I baptize with water, but among you stands one you do not know, even he who comes after me, the strap of whose sandal I am not worthy to untie" (vv. 26b–27).

Then Jesus arrived, and John declared, "Behold, the Lamb of God!" (v. 36b). He funneled everyone's excitement to Jesus. For a while, John the Baptist slipped into the background of John's gospel. Jesus was on the scene. Jesus was preaching the kingdom of God. Jesus was baptizing disciples. Jesus was becoming famous.

This bothered some of John's followers. They were thinking what I'd grown up thinking: this world is about popularity, reputation, and making a name for yourself. They were bothered, not for John, but because they had hoped John's fame would be the path to their own. The stakes were high *for them*. "John, this Jesus is stealing the glory you've earned for us—that is, for yourself. He's becoming popular, and you're losing fans. The smaller you get, the tinier we become."

That's my paraphrase of what John records in 3:26: "They came to John and said to him, 'Rabbi, he who was with you across the Jordan, to whom you bore witness—look, he is baptizing, and all are going to him.'"

What John the Baptist said in response gave me a new vision for my life. John said about Jesus' arrival and growing fame: "Therefore this joy of mine is now complete. He must increase, but I must decrease" (vv. 29b–30).

Why would John the Baptist choose to see the name and reputation of Christ increase and his name and reputation decrease?

First, it was entirely appropriate. John wasn't the Messiah, and he knew it. But the answer is more personal for John than that: John knew that nothing makes a heart shrivel faster than pride. He knew the addictive, destructive nature of seeking his glory.

It's the fallen human condition: We like to hear our names celebrated. We want to see our names on trophies, in record books, and up in lights. The more we see and hear our names, the more we develop an appetite to see and hear our names. Like unchecked weeds in a garden, pride competes for the space in our hearts that the worship of Jesus should hold. Soon, the glory of our name is the only thing we seek. John knew that seeking his glory would give him a small, miserable life.

He wanted peace. He wanted a contented soul. He knew that the path of life is enjoyed by those who seek God's glory, not their own. It's not enough to say that John was unbothered by losing followers to Jesus. He described the experience as his "joy" being "now complete."

The vision of Christ's glory and fame freed John from that tiny life. About two thousand years later, the same vision released me from my small life.

Are you, my friend, liberated by the gospel to seek the glory, fame, and reputation of Jesus alone?

QUESTIONS FOR FURTHER REFLECTION:

1. What are some ways you try to elevate your reputation in the eyes of others?
2. Do you struggle when others' accomplishments get recognized above your own? Why?
3. How can you continually remind yourself to seek the glory and reputation of Jesus instead of your own?

23

HOPE FOR MONSTERS

It is nearly as hard for a sinner to recognize the world's temptations as it is for a fish to discover impurities in the water.

Eugene Peterson, *A Long Obedience in the Same Direction*

Scripture to Read: Luke 15:11–32; 1 John 1:6–10

There's an area of the San Juan River that I declared I'd never fish again. In the way that food poisoning ruins your taste for the dish that brought it on, a phone call soured my stomach to one of my favorite casting spots.

The call came during a vacation several years ago with my good friend and pastoral colleague Nathan. We were drifting nymph rigs through the riffles when Nathan's phone rang. He couldn't make out every word, so he walked up a hill to get a stronger signal. When he started down the hill about an hour later, his shoulders slumped as if a weight had been set upon them.

It had. The call was from a mutual friend: a husband, father of two young sons, and business owner in a neighboring community. Our friend had been cheating on his wife with an old girlfriend. Minutes after the woman made their secret known, our friend called Nathan for help.

The poet and essayist Michel de Montaigne writes, "I have never seen greater monster or miracle in the world than myself."[21]

Monsters are real. One of them called to confess he'd had an affair. One of them is writing this devotional. And no offense, but one of them is reading it.

Each of us is born in sin, and though many of us have been saved by grace through faith in Jesus, we still sin and hurt the people we love. We still say hurtful things, spend our money selfishly, and let our pride tear our relationships apart. Sometimes, as with this friend, we do truly awful things to the people we most love. To deny we sin as Christians, John writes, is to "deceive ourselves" (1 John 1:8b).

Our offenses against God and others sink us into dark places of shame and isolation. They ruin our experience of fellowship with God, which is the very joy of our salvation. Our sins tempt us to think that there isn't hope, that we've sunk so low that even God can't save us. Or won't.

But there is hope! Just as monsters are real, so are miracles. By miracles, I mean the fresh giving of God's grace and mercy. Even monsters can be forgiven and restored. John also writes, "If we confess our sins, he is faithful and just to forgive us our sins and to cleanse us from all unrighteousness" (v. 9).

We take our first step in our walk with God by trusting in Jesus' death and resurrection. How do we, who are saints who still sin, move forward from then on? We remain on step one. There is no second step. When we sin, we return to the message that Jesus' death on the cross pays for our sins and His life makes us righteous. We cling to the same gospel that saved us, for it is the good news that cleanses our hearts when we do monstrous things.

Not all those who commit adultery are crushed by the weight of their sin and driven to true repentance. And only some of those spouses who were wronged by such a painful offense choose to stay married. It seems like a miracle of God's doing when either person responds that way. It feels like two miracles when both make those choices.

All praise to God, because both miracles happened in our friend's situation. His sin did crush him in an appropriate and holy way, and his wife did choose the long, arduous journey toward restoration. When Nathan and I returned from Colorado, we began counseling our friend and his wife. For several months, we returned to the principle of the grace of God that gives us the freedom to tell the truth, own up to our sins, and forgive those who have wronged us. We prayed without ceasing, asking that the power of God would heal what man had all but killed.

That phone call in the river occurred about a decade ago. I'm thankful to report that our friend and his wife are still married. They walk in truth and love today in a way they'd never known.

In his song "Don't You Want to Thank Someone," Andrew Peterson wonders how, in a world in which so many things go wrong, we still see beauty and truth. I appreciate that song because I wonder at God's grace all the time. I wonder why God gave so much back to my friend, his wife, and their sons. I wonder why a home that should have blown up like a hand grenade has become a warm, safe shelter. I wonder why He gave Nathan and me the privilege of front-row seats to see His work of restoring a marriage.

I also wonder why God took a once-wrecked fishing spot and gave it a new appeal. Because He did that too. Last summer, I returned to the San Juan. As I drove toward the water, I recalled the beautiful gifts

God has given to our friends. As I considered how He gives miracles to monsters, I thought about that fishing spot differently. The place that had symbolized my friend's unfaithfulness now seemed like a monument to God's faithfulness. I wanted to be there. When I arrived, I waded into the river precisely where I'd been standing when Nathan got the call.

My brother or sister, if you're in a dark place because of a deep or long-standing sin, it probably feels like God is far away. I'm guessing it feels like you're too dirty for Him and He's turned His back on you. That's what your enemy wants you to think. The truth is that God hasn't left you. You've moved away from Him, but He's still there. He still loves you.

From one monster to another, trust me: there is a miracle waiting for you. You're a confession away from sweet communion with God.

QUESTIONS FOR FURTHER REFLECTION:

1. Do you have a secret sin that immediately comes to mind as you read this devotion? Has keeping it hidden brought you joy, life, and peace? If not, what should you do?
2. Who would be a safe, trusted friend whom you could confess that sin to? Is there anything keeping you from finding the miracle of mercy through the confession of sin?
3. Have you seen someone restored from a hurtful sin? In what ways did that experience encourage your faith?

24

THE JOY OF HUMILITY

Some forest streams
Are amazed to be noticed. Rivers, the big ones, are sure
They deserve it. Only the ocean pays no
Attention, being past all that.

Robert Bly, "The Ocean Rising and Falling"

Scripture to Read: Isaiah 45:7–9; Philippians 2:1–11

The only signs of our encounter with the bull shark were two kneeprints in the sand near the shoreline. Our family had rented a house on St. George Island in late March. Florida is the perfect remedy for bodies and minds craving vitamin D after a long Midwest winter. Seasonal affective disorder is real. So is the rejuvenating power of the sun's rays as they strike the embarrassingly white skin of a pastor from Nebraska.

After lunch on our third day of vacation, I took up my usual post: a folding chair by the ocean. I overlooked four fishing rods rigged with shrimp that I'd cast beyond the breakers. There's a thrill to ocean fishing from the beach—when a rod tip bounces, you have no idea what kind of fish is at the end of your line. So far that week, I'd caught jack, sheepshead, flounder, mackerel, and several sand sharks.

What I most wanted that afternoon was a pompano. I'd watched our neighbor catch one while our family ate lunch on the deck. She had filleted the fish, putting the translucent meat into a bowl, and then she had thrown the carcass back into the ocean. Having seen her success, I finished lunch quickly, grabbed the poles and pole holders, and raced to the shoreline to catch one for myself.

My daughter Kate, who was ten at the time, and her cousin joined me on the beach. My fishing rods were fourteen feet long, and the lines entered the ocean thirty yards from the beach, allowing Kate and her cousin plenty of room to play in the shallows in front of my chair.

Moments after we'd settled in, as I stared at the tips of my rods, I heard screaming behind me. I looked back toward the house and saw my mom, dad, and Jamie jumping up and down and frantically pointing to their right. That's when I finally realized what they were saying: "Shark! There's a shark coming! Grab the kids!"

Jamie told me afterward that from the second-floor porch where they'd been sitting, the six-foot bull shark swimming down the shoreline toward Kate and her cousin looked like a black torpedo.

I spun around and looked at the children. I saw a large black fin about three feet from my daughter and getting closer. Terror gripped my entire body. My chest felt like it was in a vise. I raced into the ocean to grab the children.

I watched the shark pause next to Kate as if trying to decide whether to bite, circle, or swim down the coast. By the grace of God, it chose the latter, and nobody got hurt. I grabbed both kids and hustled them to dry land.

Safe on shore, hearts pounding and knees quivering from adrenaline, the three of us watched the bull shark swim to the filleted pompano remains. It snatched the carcass, made a ninety-degree turn, and swam into the depths of the Gulf of Mexico.

At that moment, my family reached the beach at a full sprint. Kate jumped into Jamie's arms, and my nephew flew into my sister's. I dropped to my knees in the sand and prayed. It was an emotional prayer—I was still in shock: "Thank You, God! Thank You!"

One of the secrets to a happy life is humility. It's the state of being so captured by the greatness of God that we're free from thinking about ourselves.

On the plane ride home a few days later, I scrolled through our vacation photos on my phone. I noticed something. While I was smiling in all the images (a beach vacation will do that), my smiles were more prominent in the hours *following* the shark encounter. The photos told the truth: the entire trip had been enjoyable, but the moments after the near miss were my happiest ones. From the time I held Kate in my arms in the surf to when I fell asleep that night to the sound of the waves, I felt lighter. Consumed with gratitude toward God. It was as if my worries had followed that shark out to the depths of the sea.

One of the secrets to a happy life is humility. It's the state of being so captured by the greatness of God that we're free from thinking about ourselves. In his book *Humility*, Gavin Ortlund writes, "Humility opens our eyes to the wonders all around us: it is sensitivity to reality, the turning of our narrow selves to the vast ocean of externality, and ultimately to God himself. In this way, humility is, in every circumstance, the key to joy, flourishing, and life itself."[22]

We don't need to be in the aftermath of a near-death experience to have the "joy, flourishing, and life itself" that humility offers. We can choose to read the Scriptures each day and meditate on God's infinite nature. When we "turn [our] eyes upon Jesus," as one of our hymns suggests, "the things of earth will grow strangely dim."[23]

There are numerous doctrines we can study as we ask the Spirit to give us the joy of humility. We can consider God's sovereignty and governance over all things, as seen in Isaiah 45: "I form light and create darkness; I make well-being and create calamity; I am the LORD, who does all these things" (v. 7).

We can meditate on Jesus, the Word of God, as our creator and sustainer, as suggested in Colossians 1:16–17, "For by him all things were created, in heaven and on earth, visible and invisible, whether thrones or dominions or rulers or authorities—all things were created through him and for him. And he is before all things, and in him all things hold together."

We can focus on the humility of Christ, as Paul describes in Philippians 2: Jesus "who, though he was in the form of God, did not count equality with God a thing to be grasped, but emptied himself, by taking the form of a servant, being born in the likeness of men" (vv. 6–7).

Genuine humility and gratitude are the fountains of happiness in the heart of a Christian. We don't need to encounter a crisis or nearly escape a tragedy to enjoy these daily pleasures. We have the Spirit of

God wielding the sword of the Word (see Eph. 6:17). He can penetrate our hearts and give us these joys every day.

Though I felt happiest on the day of the shark encounter, I was also delighted the following morning. While sipping my first cup of coffee, one of my rod tips bounced. I put the mug in the cupholder and reeled in my line. A bright and shiny pompano, the color of unwrinkled tinfoil, splashed in the ocean before me.

I filleted the fish and placed the translucent meat into a bowl. The carcass? I tossed it into a trash can by the house.

QUESTIONS FOR FURTHER REFLECTION:

1. What passages or doctrines do you like to study when you seek to be humbled and delighted by the greatness of God?
2. How do you recognize when you're spending too much time thinking about yourself or your worries? Do your friends or family members help you recognize those moments?
3. Do you ever pray through a passage of Scripture? That is a great way to engage your heart and mind in your worship of God through His Word. Let me encourage you to read and pray through one right now.

25

COMPANIONABLE CREATURES

Slowly we became silent, and silence itself is an enemy to friendship.

Norman Maclean, *A River Runs through It*

Scripture to Read: Romans 12:1–13; Hebrews 10:23–25

I tossed my wader boots, caked with sand from the Au Sable River, into the trunk of my rental car. The first leg of my trip had ended, and it was time to meet up with friends for a day of charter fishing on Lake Huron for trout and salmon.

I'd spent the first four days in Michigan by myself, fishing the "Holy Waters" section of the Au Sable. I stayed in a one-room cabin. I bought groceries for one, cooked for one, and cleaned up a mess in the kitchen each night that only one person had made. I didn't even see another soul while fishing. The Au Sable twists and turns throughout the Lower Peninsula, and if there were other anglers around the bend during my times on the river, I didn't see them.

I'd intentionally been alone those first four days. I wanted to work on this book. I also hoped to sort through my thoughts and clear some clutter from my mind. But as the week went on, I felt more and more lonely. In fact, on the third afternoon, I did something I don't typically do when fishing: I took a break. I sat on the riverbank, pulled out my phone, and scrolled through photos of my family and friends. I laughed out loud, even talked to myself, none of which embarrassed me because nobody was there to hear it.

At the end of the fourth day, I headed east to meet up with friends. We got up early the next morning, drove to Lake Huron, and boarded a fishing charter. For eight hours, the five of us took turns landing lake trout, steelhead, and salmon—filling the cooler with twenty-one massive fish—before returning to Butch's home in Posen, Michigan.

When we entered the house, Butch's sister Lisa was in the kitchen making us dinner. If there's anything better than the sound of bacon sizzling in a cast-iron pan, it's the smell of bacon when it sucker punches you as you enter the house. When the bacon was crisp, Lisa mixed it with sautéed mushrooms and ricotta cheese, then tucked portions of the mixture into folds of homemade dough. The pierogi went back into the pan, and Lisa poured butter and cream sauce over the entire dish. We feasted like Vikings returning from a raid.

We were made for community. We need relationships in order to flourish. Herman Bavinck writes, "Solitude is poverty, forsakenness, gradual pining and wasting away. How lonesome it is to be alone!"[24]

This need for companionship can be traced back to the original good state. In Genesis 2, we find Adam in a place of perfection and beauty. There was no mold on the fruit. No thorns on the ground. It was a simply perfect environment, yet something was missing. Adam was lonely, and God said, "It is not good that the man should be alone" (v. 18a).

The creation narrative shows us that God is always and only good. It also teaches us that God, as a relational being, created us in His image to need and enjoy relationships. Genesis also shows us that God delights in meeting our need for relationships through other people. When God gave Adam the sweet gift of Eve, He intentionally put Adam to sleep. I imagine this was partly to spare Adam the pain of having a rib removed. However, the deeper reason for this narrative detail, I suspect, is to show us how Adam's need for companionship was met by God alone. Adam was asleep. He did nothing. Eve, by definition, was a gift.

We're tempted to believe that to be free and happy, we must be able to move in or out of any group we choose, even the church. No strong ties. Nothing holding us down.

This helps us understand the gift God gives us in the church. When we trust in Christ, God places us into the priesthood of all believers (see 1 Pet. 2:5), the body of Christ. As Adam received Eve as a gift, so we should receive one another, brothers and sisters in Christ, by the grace of God alone. We are a gift from God to one another.

Yet if we're honest, we might need to admit that we don't always want this gift. Some may even need to acknowledge that they have fought against receiving this gift. We're inclined to think of ourselves, even as Christians, as isolated, autonomous people. We're tempted to believe that to be free and happy, we must be able to move in or out of any group we choose, even the church. No strong ties. Nothing holding us down.

This is a joy-stealing mindset. One of the clearest themes I've identified in twenty-five years of ministry and counseling is that the most miserable, lonely Christians are those who have ruggedly asserted their autonomy from a local church. They're as sad as Adam would've been had he looked at Eve and said, "Thanks, but no thanks."

The church is God's gift to us that we might belong. God has given me to you. He has given you to me.

Sebastian Junger, in his book *Tribe*, presents a strong case for a sense of belonging as one of the human heart's most essential, vital needs. He interviewed people who experienced war and natural disasters, comparing mental health during times of hardship versus times of peace and prosperity. He concludes, "Humans don't mind hardship, in fact they thrive on it; what they mind is not feeling necessary. Modern society has perfected the art of making people not feel necessary. It is time for that to end."[25]

Junger has simply discovered what the Bible teaches from start to finish: We were made to belong to one another. We were made to be a part of something larger, more demanding and satisfying than merely our solitary lives. The church is God's gift to us that we might belong. God has given me to you. He has given you to me. He's given us a family, as the psalmist writes: "God settles the solitary in a home" (Ps. 68:6a).

Later that evening, with bellies full of bacon and butter, my friends and I gathered around the firepit in Butch's backyard. A deep happiness settled upon me. The isolation of the first four days had, I'm confident, enhanced my enjoyment of fellowship that evening. Being alone helped me appreciate being together. These friends were a gift.

QUESTIONS FOR FURTHER REFLECTION:

1. What are some of the challenging parts of committing to a particular community of faith through thick and thin?
2. What are some of the gifts your community might miss out on if you weren't a part of it?
3. What keeps you from making even deeper commitments to your community with your time, talents, and resources?

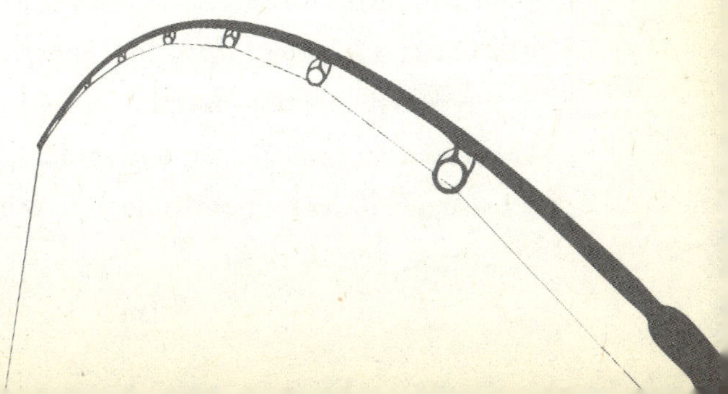

26

THE WAY OF FRIENDS

The mighty rivers of America have been vulgarized by commerce, glamorized by legend and song. Acts of the national drama have played across their stages. They have determined battles, fostered grand engineering projects, and fomented disasters.

Norm Bomer, *Sons of the River: A Nebraska Memoir*

Scripture to Read: Job 1:1–22; 42:1–17; John 15:9–15

Nothing ruins a fishing trip faster than a fight between friends. It was the first day of our college spring break, and two friends and I were fishing one of Nebraska's state lakes. As often happens, one angler was more successful than the other two. As I recall, after he had landed yet another black crappie, our successful friend playfully bragged about his skills as an angler.

What he meant to be funny wasn't received that way by the angler having a slow day and who was, by that point, extremely frustrated. He responded by giving evidence as to why, despite his current lousy luck, he was, in fact, the better fisherman. The first angler took offense, and his words ceased sounding playful.

This conflict occurred so long ago and the issue was so trivial that I struggle to remember the details. What I do remember with clarity is that the trek from the far side of the lake back to the boat ramp was excruciatingly painful. The Nebraska Game and Parks Commission had declared that entire body of water to be a "no-wake lake," which meant we couldn't drive faster than ten miles an hour. That speed is a delight when everyone's getting along. But when you can cut the tension with a fillet knife, it feels like a new level in Dante's Inferno.

The book of Job is a reminder that friendships are difficult. At the beginning of the book, God declares that Job is a righteous man. Satan challenged God, suggesting that Job did the right things only because God had been good to him. Satan said, "Stretch out your hand and touch all that he has, and he will curse you to your face" (1:11).

> **There is a type of friendship that merely gives others access to our posts on social media but leaves us lonely. We want brotherhood and sisterhood. We want to belong to others.**

God permitted Satan to strike Job despite the fact that Job was righteous. Job's sufferings weren't the just punishment or direct outcome of his sins. This is where Job's three friends went sideways. They arrived after Satan had attacked Job. They were shocked by Job's loss. We're told, "They sat with him on the ground seven days and seven nights, and no one spoke a word to him, for they saw that his suffering was very great" (2:13). They entered their friend's grief. This was a good start. Their silence likely encouraged Job.

Once they started talking, however, they deeply wounded their friend. They spiritualized Job's situation, insisting that his sin had caused the Lord's wrath. The more they talked, the more their words became yet another catastrophe for Job to endure.

At the end of the story, God rebukes Job's friends. The text tells us the heart of their failure as friends: they misrepresented God. Listen to what God said to Eliphaz, one of Job's friends: "My anger burns against you and against your two friends, *for you have not spoken of me what is right*, as my servant Job has" (42:7b).

They hurt Job by speaking lies about God. They not only believed they were right, but they also assumed God was on their side. "Job, you should listen to us. We're speaking for God."

The friends we desire are ones ... who make us feel safe and loved when we confess our sins. The friends we need are those who won't just say, "I'll pray for you"—they *will* pray for you.

Jesus is the perfect contrast to Job's friends. In John 15:15, He said to His disciples, "No longer do I call you servants, for the servant does not know what his master is doing; but I have called you friends, for all that I have heard from my Father I have made known to you."

At the end of that statement, Jesus explained why He'd called them friends: "For all that I have heard from my Father I have made known to you." What makes someone a friend? What changed the disciples from Jesus' "servants" to His friends? Jesus let them in on who He was and what He was doing.

Jesus was a faithful friend by giving Himself to others. He spoke what was true about Himself, and He spoke what was true about God. He did this to draw His friends close to Him and to draw them close to God.

Eliphaz, Bildad, and Zophar failed to be Job's friends when they shared simplistic, false ideas about God. They didn't draw Job near to them, nor did they help Job draw near to God. Their false representation of God pushed their friend away from them and played an instrumental role in Job's doubt about the fairness of his Creator.

Friends allow one another into the deepest aspects of their lives: who they are, what they're doing, what they think, feel, and believe. Friends also speak the truth about God for the purpose of helping one another draw near to their Father in heaven. Pastor T. J. Tims described the unique opportunity Christians have for finding this kind of friendship. In a discussion with his friend Sam Allberry, Pastor Tims said:

> We as Christians are just in such a great position for friendship. Because what's deepest in my heart, Christ Himself, my best friend, is also your best friend, and when you and I get together and go deep in that way, it's possible to create deep friendships very quickly.[26]

We long for this kind of friendship. There is a type of friendship that merely gives others access to our posts on social media but leaves us lonely. We want brotherhood and sisterhood. We want to belong to others. The friends we desire are ones we can call without texting to ask permission first. They're the ones who make us feel safe and loved when we confess our sins. The friends we need are those who won't just say, "I'll pray for you"—they *will* pray for you. These are the friends we want, and they are a gift from God when we find them.

Even Christian friendships can be difficult, as my two friends illustrated that day on the boat. They didn't speak to each other for several months after that outing. I remained hopeful. I knew both men loved Jesus. I also knew the story of Job and how God restored Job's friends to him at the end of the book.

Eventually, my friends did sit down and talk things out. They forgave each other, and it wasn't long before the three of us made our way across that same state lake at the blazing speed of ten miles an hour.

QUESTIONS FOR FURTHER REFLECTION:

1. Think about a time when a friend ministered to you deeply during a period of suffering. What did they do that encouraged you? How did they point you to the truth?
2. When you are trying to help a friend who is suffering, how do you know when to be silent and when to speak?
3. Have you ever committed the error of Job's friends? If so, did God humble you and restore your friendship? If that hasn't happened yet, why not?

27

THE GOOD, IMPERFECT GIFT

[The Mole said:] "Do you know, I've never been in a boat before in all my life."

"What?" cried the Rat, open-mouthed: "Never been in a—you never—well I—what have you been doing, then?"

"Is it so nice as all that?" asked the Mole shyly....

"Nice? It's the only thing," said the Water Rat solemnly, as he leant forward for his stroke. "Believe me, my young friend, there is nothing—absolutely nothing—half so much worth doing as simply messing about in boats. Simply messing," he went on dreamily: "messing—about—in—boats; messing—"

Kenneth Grahame, *The Wind in the Willows*

Scripture to Read: Romans 12

Several years ago, I chartered a boat in Baja to fish for grouper, halibut, and sea bass. The captain met me at the dock near our cabin and walked me to his boat. It was a long boat with a modified V hull and a center console for the captain. It looked sleek and stable, with plenty of room to cast and net fish. As I stepped from the dock into the craft, I felt the thrill of possibility.

"I know, it's a piece of junk," the captain said. "I just hope it gets us through the morning."

For five hours, the boat's owner complained about one aspect of his vessel after another. It wasn't long enough. It didn't have a toilet. The motor didn't have enough power. The fiberglass was dull and cracked. We caught fish that morning, but my ever-growing fears of sinking overshadowed the thrill of the catch. I was glad when the trip was over. Stepping from the boat onto the dock, I felt lucky to have survived my time at sea.

I fished from the shoreline the following day, just a stone's throw from the dock and the boat. Between casts, I watched that boat lift and fall with the waves. It didn't appear junky or old, but rather solid and graceful. Its bow faced the ocean as if eager for its next appointment with the sea. The longer I watched, my opinion of the boat reverted to my first impression before its owner had verbally torn it apart.

I soon felt foolish for letting the captain pull me into his negativity toward his vessel. That craft had provided safe passage through several miles of breaking waves and ocean swells. It'd given me a firm foundation from which to cast, fight, and net good-sized fish. My family ate a delicious halibut meal that night because that boat had come through for us. Watching it later, free from the critical comments of its owner, I wished I could relive the previous morning with my new perspective.

I'm not sure I know of any organization in America that receives more verbal punishment than the church. Some negativity comes from those who don't believe in God. That shouldn't be a surprise—Jesus promised that the world would hate Christians. What is shocking, however, is how popular it has become for Christians to criticize the body of Christ and cast aside their local churches.

In 1 Timothy 3:15, Paul calls the church "the household of God" and "a pillar and buttress of the truth." A local church consisting of quirky saints is *the house of the living God*. Jesus said, "For where two or three are gathered in my name, there am I among them" (Matt. 18:20). Gathered Christians are the living room of God, and God Himself is there with them.

I'm not suggesting we stop seeking growth or change within our local churches. No church is perfect, which means there will always be room for prayerful discernment from committed Christians. What's more, some churches need to change in dramatic ways to be faithful to Christ. The Spirit of God gives wisdom and courage to each generation to examine, critique, and call their churches to greater faithfulness. Most of the letters in the New Testament were written for this purpose, and churches haven't stopped needing watchful scrutiny since.

But that examination, critique, and calling back to Christ is very different from the "I love Jesus, but I've given up on the church" attitude that is faddish today. The first thinks, speaks, and acts from the doctrine that Jesus died on the cross to form the church. The latter believes the lie that Christians can please Jesus while tearing down His body.

To be clear, I don't write this devotion to protect the church. The church doesn't need my protection; it will grow and thrive throughout all generations. Jesus said, "The gates of hell shall not prevail against it" (Matt. 16:18b).

Rather, my aim is our joy. I write this because I want us to have the pleasure of thanksgiving that springs from gratitude toward the boat we're in. God saved us and placed us into His body. We are a part of the body of Christ, and we experience this primarily through our local church. Our local church is our boat, and it's an immeasurable gift from God.

Yet, like the captain in Baja, we can be pessimistic and cynical toward our boat even while it's keeping us afloat. We can maintain a sour attitude toward the very group of people Jesus died to give us as a gift. We can spend all our time looking for flaws. And as the boat owner did with me, we can convince others to join us in our disdain for the family of God. Dietrich Bonhoeffer describes this type of boat-owner Christian in his book *Life Together*:

> The man who fashions a visionary ideal of community demands that it be realized by God, by others, and by himself. He enters the community of Christians with his demands, sets up his own law, and judges the brethren and God himself accordingly. He stands adamant, a living reproach to all others in the circle of brethren. He acts as if he is the creator of the Christian community, as if his dream binds men together. When things do not go his way, he calls the effort a failure. When his ideal picture is destroyed, he sees the community going to smash. So he becomes, first an accuser of his brethren, then an accuser of God, and finally the despairing accuser of himself.[27]

We ruin our happiness and gratitude with this attitude toward our local church. We are the ones who lose the most. I spent my hard-earned money on the chance to fish in one of the most beautiful places in the world. I even caught fish. Yet the mindset I carried soured the gifts that the morning gave. The boat did its job. It was my attitude that failed.

As the psalmist writes, there is joy and pleasure with God: "In your presence there is fullness of joy; at your right hand are pleasures forevermore" (Ps. 16:11b).

His presence is in His house, the quirky, imperfect, incredible gift of the gathered saints in our local churches.

"Lord, help us learn to love our boats. Amen."

QUESTIONS FOR FURTHER REFLECTION:

1. How have you been critical of your "boat," your local church? How does speaking that criticism aloud affect your gratitude for the provision of the family of faith that God has given you?
2. What are three things you are grateful for as you consider your church? Consider sharing these three things with a friend or pastor.
3. What is something that your church could focus on or change to be more faithful to Jesus? I challenge you to pray each day this week for your church to grow and flourish in that area.

28

A THIEF IN THE BUILDING

That ancient hooks would still function so well is a testament to the simplicity of the contract between man and fish: bait a crooked piece of metal, tie it to a line, and cast it out. Worms work well for bottom-feeders like the carp, but if the fish preys on winged insects skating the surface, like the trout, it helps to tie a couple feathers to the hook.

Kirk Wallace Johnson, *The Feather Thief*

Scripture to Read: Ephesians 6:10–20

One evening in June 2009, the guards at the British Museum of Natural History had no idea they were being robbed. While they sipped coffee, a thief entered the ornithology collection and bagged 299 rare bird skins from sixteen species. The thief was a twenty-year-old American named Edwin Rist, a student at the Royal Conservatory of Music in London. Rist entered the museum by breaking a window on the second floor. When he had what he wanted, he slipped out of the museum, boarded a train, and returned to his apartment with his loot.

Rist made thousands of dollars selling skins from the stolen birds. However, he didn't do it for the money. His desire to own the feathers compelled him. In addition to being a musical prodigy, Rist was obsessed with tying exotic salmon flies. He was a member of an elite fly-crafting community that tied flies made from feathers from the rarest birds according to old Victorian patterns. The flies this group tied were considered works of art, some selling for several hundred dollars apiece.

By the nineteenth century, however, the group lost access to the feathers they needed. In his book *The Feather Thief*, Kirk Wallace Johnson describes how Rist and his crew were "marooned in the wrong century ... [and] dedicated to an art form that could no longer be legally practiced without great difficulty."[28]

The "great difficulty" didn't deter Rist—neither did the illegality. His lust to have what he didn't own was more than enough motivation to do the work to commit the crime.

In Ephesians 6, Paul tells us to stand firm because we are in a battle against the Devil. Satan and his spiritual forces of evil are relentless in their plans to destroy God's people. Likewise, Peter warns, "Be sober-minded; be watchful. Your adversary the devil prowls around like a roaring lion, seeking someone to devour" (1 Pet. 5:8).

If Satan can make us think he's not real or not a threat, he's got us where he wants us: in the dark and unaware.

What motivates Satan to hunt?

His lust to have what he cannot own.

From the time God cast Satan from heaven (see Isa. 14:12) until today, the Devil has wanted what belongs to God. He's wanted God's glory. He's wanted God's worship. He's wanted God's people. He knows his time is short, so he's furiously committed. Revelation states, "Woe to you, O earth and sea, for the devil has come down to you in great wrath, because he knows that his time is short!" (12:12b).

What's Satan's caper, and how is he carrying it out?

As the Father of Lies (see John 8:44), Satan's strategy is to trick us into believing what isn't true—that people are our enemy, not him, or that we're not actually in a spiritual battle. There's nothing Satan would like more than to deceive God's people into believing, despite Paul's words in Ephesians 6, that he isn't trying to steal our devotion to God. If he can make us think he's not real or not a threat, he's got us where he wants us: in the dark and unaware.

In Ephesians 6, Paul lists six parts of the armor of God, so we will know how to stand against our enemy:

1. *The belt of truth (v. 14)*: Soldiers wore belts to hold their clothing tight to their bodies so they could move quickly. As Jesus lived and spoke only what was true, we stand against the Devil by walking in integrity and truthfulness.
2. *The breastplate of righteousness (v. 14)*: The breastplate was the armor that protected a soldier's heart and other vital organs. As Jesus walked rightly before God and mankind, we can stand against the Devil by honoring and obeying the Lord and loving our neighbor as ourselves.
3. *The "readiness given by the gospel of peace" shoes (v. 15)*: Shoes allowed the soldiers to race toward

their intended goal. By His life, death, and resurrection, Jesus gave peace to Jews and Gentiles, men and women, old and young. So we stand against the Devil by racing to others to ask for forgiveness or grant forgiveness so that we might live in unity.

4. *The shield of faith (v. 16)*: A soldier's shield protected his entire body from the arrows of an opposing army. We stand against the Devil by trusting in every word and promise of God, especially the truth that Jesus secured our enemy's defeat at the cross.
5. *The helmet of salvation (v. 17)*: The helmet protected the soldier's head, and thus his mind, the arena where battles begin and are won or lost. We stand against Satan by constantly thinking about the beauties of our salvation. "For by grace you have been saved through faith. And this is not your own doing; it is the gift of God" (Eph. 2:8). When we're meditating on God's grace, we're not entertaining Satan's lies.
6. *The sword of the Spirit, the Word of God (v. 17)*: This is the one offensive weapon that Paul lists, and it's a weapon for destruction and death. When Satan tempted Jesus in the wilderness, Jesus stood against him by remembering, quoting, and trusting the Scriptures. We stand against the Devil by doing the same thing.

Rist's crime was so sneaky that it took the British Museum a month to even realize they'd been robbed. It took law enforcement an additional eighteen months to apprehend Rist.

Ironically, as they looked worldwide for suspects, the thief's name had been under their noses the entire time. Months before the crime, Rist had posed as a photographer to examine the room and hatch a plan. He'd signed his actual name on the ornithology room's guest list, proving how, if people aren't looking in the right direction, not even a name on paper will foil the crime.

We have our enemy's name in ink. We must resist him by walking in the wisdom, character, and integrity of Jesus. Let us pray at all times, without ceasing, for ourselves and one another, as Paul writes, "Finally, be strong in the Lord and in the strength of his might" (Eph. 6:10).

The Devil can't have us. We belong to Christ.

QUESTIONS FOR FURTHER REFLECTION:

1. How does Satan tempt you to believe that God is not actually good or that He will not do what He promised He would? How has the Devil tricked you into thinking that you know better than God what will make you happy?
2. Jesus combated temptation with Scripture. What is a passage you could memorize and trust in those times when you face Satan's attack?
3. How does knowing you belong to Jesus, and not Satan, give you strength to stand against the attacks of the Evil One?

29

BLUE FLIES

The Old Angler also ministered efficiently to the souls of men, was a delightful companion, and a persistent fisherman. He had no fixed period for his vacation but went fishing whenever the spirit moved him, or, in other words, about three times a week.

Charles Lose, *The Vanishing Trout*

Scripture to Read: Luke 12:29–34; 1 Timothy 6:6–19

It was the first time I'd seen grown men wildly excited about the color blue. I was on a weeklong sabbatical from ministry. In the mornings, I read and journaled. In the afternoons, I fly fished Lake Taneycomo, the reservoir on the back side of Table Rock Lake. I was positioned a couple of hundred feet from the Powersite Dam ...

And having absolutely no success. I tried dozens of flies, added and subtracted weight, and experimented with various depths by moving my indicator, but I couldn't get a hit. What made things worse was that I could see fish. Several trout were hovering a few feet downriver in the murky wake my wader boots created.

"Morning, friend!"

I turned to see a couple of older gentlemen walking down the footpath from the parking area. Someone once said that every tall person needs a short friend, and if that's true, then these men were clearly meant to be best buds. For the final step from the trees to the riverbank, a two-foot drop, the taller man offered his hand to the shorter one. The shorter man took it, saying, "Always rubbing it in that you're taller, Fred."

When they reached me, the shorter gentleman introduced himself as Roger. He said, "We don't mean to bother you, but we were eating lunch at the truck and noticed that you weren't catching much. Would you like a few tips?"

I gladly welcomed their help, even more so their conversation. It turned out that Roger and Fred had been lifelong friends. They'd met in kindergarten in a small town in southern Arkansas. Though they relentlessly teased one another, their words had a genteel Southern politeness and charm.

"You got anything blue in your fly box?" Fred asked.

I didn't. I'd never fished with blue flies before. Purple, sure. Even pink and red, but never blue. If you'd given me an entire year to stand on the banks of Taneycomo and try new ideas, blue flies would never have crossed my mind.

When they saw my blank expression, both men reached for their fly boxes as if they were drawing pistols to see who was quicker. When they opened them, all I saw was blue. Aqua, baby blue, navy, cobalt—you name it, they had it. I hadn't seen that much blue in one place since our son's baby shower.

They weren't just quick to draw their boxes from their bags; they also had mine in their hands before I knew what was happening. They almost seemed in competition to see who could put the most blue flies into the empty foam reams in my boxes. When they finished, I had easily three dozen new imitation midges, scuds, worms, woolly buggers, and leeches—all blue.

When I demanded to pay, the two men seemed bothered. Roger patted me on the arm. "Your money's no good here, son. We just want to see you catch fish."

Maybe it's because I'm a pastor, so asking heart-level questions is just what I do, but their generosity stunned me, and I had to know from where it came. "All right, guys, why give three dozen flies to a perfect stranger?"

Fred went first, telling me about how someone had shared the gospel with him in his twenties. "Jesus changed my life," he said. "I went from wanting to earn a lot of money to wanting to give a bunch away. Having Christ makes me want to be generous."

Roger's story was similar. In fact, Fred was the one to share Jesus with him. He, too, described how Jesus had replaced his desire to get rich with the desire to care for others.

The friends described how, years ago, just months into their Christian lives, they had made a pact. They called it their "Timothy Oath." They committed to God and to one another to be rich in good works and always generous in storing up treasure in heaven.

Roger and Fred then boldly asked me if I wanted to put my faith in Jesus. This happens all the time on the river. I'll have a great talk with another angler or two, and then they will share the gospel and invite me to give my life to Christ. I love it! I'm thrilled every time it happens. It gives me a chance to share my story of discovering the grace and mercy of God.

It also invariably leads to praying with another angler on the water. I've given thanks numerous times with various anglers across this country. When a couple of anglers discover that they don't just share a love for fly fishing but also a passion for Jesus, how can you not involve your Savior in the dialogue?

Thanks to Roger and Fred, I netted about a dozen plump rainbows that afternoon. And thanks to them, I'm wildly excited about the color blue.

QUESTIONS FOR FURTHER REFLECTION:

1. How does 2 Corinthians 8:9 encourage us to thank God and be generous to others? "For you know the grace of our Lord Jesus Christ, that though he was rich, yet for your sake he became poor, so that you by his poverty might become rich."
2. How can you use generosity as a means of practicing your trust in God's provision and kindness to you?
3. How does our generosity help us "take hold of that which is truly life," as Paul describes in 1 Timothy 6:19b?

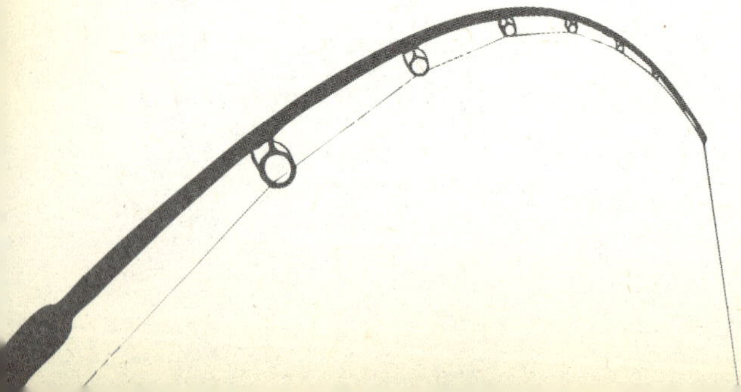

30

KEEP YOUR NET HANDY

One does nothing with a hooked rainbow for about thirty seconds. The rainbow has everything his way. He was all over the pool, under the bank, out in the open, and back to his pool before I felt I had a chance to net him.

Gordon MacQuarrie, *The Gordon MacQuarrie Sporting Treasury*

Scripture to Read: Romans 9:1–33; 2 Thessalonians 2:13–14

It's the only fish we've ever put in the boat that acted like he wanted to be there. My five-year-old son, Aidan, was fighting a sunfish. The panfish, about the size of a wide-mouthed canning lid, had Aidan's Snoopy rod bent into an extreme arch. As the fish flopped around at the water's surface, I noticed something large emerging beneath it. Whatever it was rose slowly. My first thought was that a log must have dislodged from the bottom of the lake. But as the mass neared the sunfish, it looked less like a branch and more like the gaping mouth of a giant bass.

"Buddy, look! There's a largemouth trying to swallow your sunfish!"

It was early spring, and the water in the lake was barely above freezing. The bass sluggishly struck Aidan's fish as if only slightly interested, giving me enough time to grab the net and slip it into the water below both fish. I lifted them up together and set them on the floor of the boat. We tossed the sunfish back in the water, but as you might imagine, the bass spent a little time with us.

We measured and weighed it—five pounds thirteen ounces, twenty-one-and-a-half inches long—then held it up for several photos. A couple of minutes after netting the fish, we released it and watched the behemoth swim back to the bottom in the slow, disinterested manner with which it had emerged.

When I told Aidan that his largemouth was longer than any bass I'd caught, his five-year-old chest puffed up like a down jacket. He started talking smack, describing how catching big fish seemed easier than he'd imagined.

Trying to reset his expectations, I said, "Son, I've never caught a fish like that—it's like that bass wanted to be in the boat."

One of the thrills of the Christian life is talking with people who already want to be saved by grace through faith in Christ. This is my story. When I entered my sophomore year in college, I'd gone to church only once in my life. Even then, I hadn't gone because I'd wanted to—I'd gone because a girl I liked had invited me. (I've been a pastor for nearly thirty years, and I've seen hundreds of young men stroll through the foyer of our church with the same I-like-this-gal-but-not-this-place expression on their faces.)

I grew up making fun of Christians and thinking religion was a crutch for simple-minded people. But when I started my sophomore year in college, I actually became curious about Jesus. It was as if someone had flipped a switch in my mind. Two of my friends in the dorm were Christians, and I asked them question after question about the Bible.

Because I had such a godless past, and the crass vocabulary to prove it, what happened on November 7, 1990, was a shock for them. After three hours of hanging out in a dorm room, discussing the gospel from numerous angles, one of the guys said, "Hey, it's dinnertime. We should head over to the cafeteria."

I replied, "Can I do this first?"

"Do what?" he asked.

I didn't quite know how to word it, so I said, "You know, get on my knees and believe in Jesus."

I wanted in the boat. I had to be in the boat. There was no holding me back. The three of us knelt, and I confessed my sins and declared my faith in Jesus.

Just as our family was shocked when we put that bass in the boat, my two friends were stunned by what they'd just witnessed. To this day, when I thank them for helping me become a Christian, they declare how they felt like they did nothing. One said, "We just needed to get out of the way. God had already changed your heart. We felt like spectators."

When God saves us, He places us on a mission. Whether at work, in a dorm room, or on the water, Christians are to care more about sharing the good news of Jesus Christ than about almost anything else we do. The thrilling part is that saving others—opening their eyes and stirring their hearts to trust Jesus—is *God's* work. We call this doctrine *God's effectual call*. It's a truth that is presented clearly throughout the Bible. For example, Paul writes,

> Those whom he foreknew he also predestined to be conformed to the image of his Son, in order that he might be the firstborn among many brothers. And those whom he predestined he also called, and those whom he called he also justified, and those whom he justified he also glorified. (Rom. 8:29–30)

God's plan of salvation is rooted in the past. It's been His design since before creation. There is certainly a mystery to how His sovereignty over all things, including human hearts, allows for genuine human responsibility and free will—another truth supported in the Scriptures—but there's no denying that God calls people into eternal life. He ensures that those He predestined, He calls; and those He calls, He justifies; and those He justifies, He glorifies. His plan never fails because "it depends not on human will or exertion, but on God, who has mercy" (Rom. 9:16).

I've had the privilege of being in the room with dozens of people who, like the bass on that cold spring day, longed to get in the boat as a son or daughter of God. You don't need to be a pastor to encounter moments like that; you just need to be faithful to share the gospel.

Keep your net handy!

QUESTIONS FOR FURTHER REFLECTION:

1. Can you remember when you understood the gospel and wanted to believe in Jesus with all your heart? What was that like?

2. Have you had the chance to be in the room when someone "got in the boat" by praying and trusting in Christ? How did you feel at that moment?
3. When you share your testimony and the gospel, how can you do so with the profound trust that God does the work of drawing people to Himself?

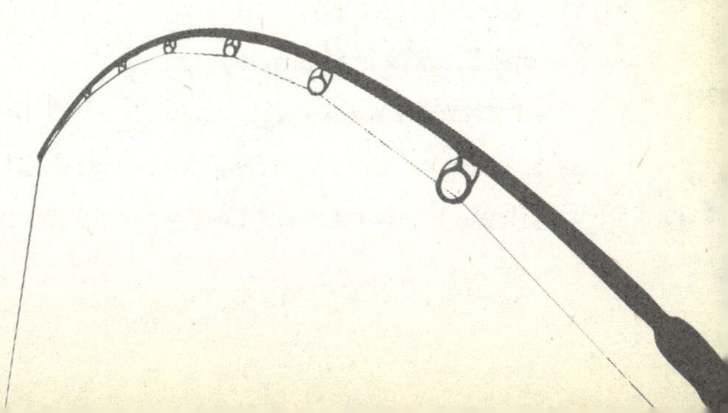

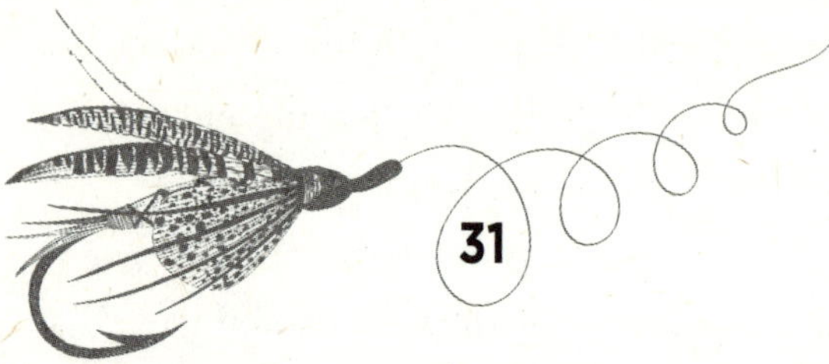

31

ALWAYS ROOM TO GROW

Fishing with somebody brings you close together because that person has a front-row seat for your failures. And those failures, if you're learning, will be frequent.

David Coggins, *The Optimist*

Scripture to Read: Proverbs 9:7–12; James 1:5–8

If given the choice, my last meal would be smoked salmon with a dill-and-cucumber chutney. Because of my culinary affection for all fish in the *Salmonidae* family, along with their reputation for fighting anglers with ferocity, I've always wanted to catch a salmon on a fly rod. That dream became a reality, thanks to the advice of a young man in Alpena, Michigan.

My friend Thom joined me for a half day of fishing in the Thunder Bay River Channel. We had only four hours to fish before our flight out of Alpena, but we donned waders and slipped into the water near the Ninth Street Dam. This stretch is famous for steelhead, coho, Chinook, and king salmon.

I started with a white leech, trying to imitate the baitfish in the system. After several casts without a strike, I went to a pheasant tail and drifted it through the fastest part of the current. Nothing hit, so I tried a golden stonefly, then a Pat's rubber legs, and then a scud with a zebra midge trailer. With thirty minutes to fish, I'd gone through all my favorite flies and was out of ideas.

I noticed a young man standing on the bank with his dog. I waved, and he waved back. I asked him if he was a local. He was. I asked him if he had any suggestions for me. He said he might, so I walked over to him. He asked me if I had any egg imitations. I did, and I opened my box to show him my trout beads and hooks. He pointed to the largest one—a fluorescent pink bead, eight millimeters in diameter—and said, "That would be perfect!"

He suggested a specific amount of weight and a precise amount of space between my first egg and my second. He showed me which part of the current to cast into. I rigged up in front of him to make sure I did exactly what he'd recommended, and then I waded out and cast to the area he'd mentioned.

On the third cast, it felt like I'd hooked an underwater passenger train. I lifted my rod tip to set the hook, and the party started. The train left the station! The fish put up a fight that was every bit as ferocious as I'd hoped it would be. Thom and the young man cheered me on. The boy occasionally made a suggestion about my drag or the angle of my rod. He was right on every time. I fought that fish for about ten minutes. It was one of the most exhilarating fishing experiences I've had to this day. The salmon eventually tired out, and when I got him to the net, I held it up for Thom and the young man to see. It was a dark, black-spotted, twenty-two-inch Chinook.

I didn't ask for advice much in my teens and twenties, and in retrospect, I undoubtedly missed out on many moments like the one in the Thunder Bay River Channel. When I was young, my goal was to prove to people what I already knew, which wasn't much. I didn't want assistance or advice; I preferred to give those things rather than receive them. In my late twenties, the book of Proverbs changed my perspective. My father-in-law, RB, challenged me to read a chapter from Proverbs each day. As I did, I gained a vision for being an advice-seeking, counsel-inviting, wisdom-wanting follower of Christ.

Proverbs offers us wisdom for every aspect of life. It also teaches us that we must want wisdom if we hope to gain it. We must choose to listen to the right voice. In Proverbs 1:20, we meet Lady Wisdom. She is the right voice. She calls aloud in the streets, raises her voice in public places, and makes herself known to those who want to hear her.

In contrast to Lady Wisdom, Proverbs introduces us to Lady Folly. Lady Folly also speaks and makes herself known. Solomon writes, "The woman Folly is loud; she is seductive and knows nothing" (9:13).

The differences between these two women are found in Proverbs 9:7–12. Those who follow Lady Folly resist advice, counsel, and instruction. They dislike anyone who tries to correct them. Their pride makes them advice givers rather than wisdom seekers. In contrast, those who follow Lady Wisdom gladly accept help and advice. They look for truth, and they treasure it when they find it.

Proverbs 9:11–12 reveals the outcome of these two ways of life. Those who listen to Lady Folly's voice, perhaps through pride or self-sufficiency, will experience the misery of foolish choices—heartache that could have been avoided. On the other hand, those who pursue instruction, correction, and wise counsel experience a vibrant life, as Lady Wisdom promises in verse 11: "For by me your days will be multiplied, and years will be added to your life."

Ultimately, what Solomon (the author of most of the book of Proverbs) is encouraging is more personal and profound than merely seeking wisdom. He's urging us to seek God, the source of all wisdom and knowledge. In Colossians 2, Paul tells us that Jesus is the wisdom of God made flesh and in Him "are hidden all the treasures of wisdom and knowledge" (v. 3b).

Let me offer a challenge that might change your life: read one chapter from Proverbs and one chapter from Matthew's gospel daily for the next thirty days. There are thirty-one chapters in Proverbs and twenty-eight chapters in Matthew, so it'll take about the same number of days. (For a thirty-day month, consider breaking chapters 26 and 27 of Matthew into two days each. Those are the longest chapters.) As you read, absorb the wisdom of Proverbs while looking for the embodiment of that wisdom in the words and deeds of Jesus.

You will see it. And you might just find yourself more thrilled by the exercise than I was to smoke that salmon and serve it to my family with my favorite dill-and-cucumber chutney recipe on the side.

QUESTIONS FOR FURTHER REFLECTION:

1. If you were to honestly assess your life, would you say you primarily pursue wisdom or follow your own heart? Let me encourage you to pray that God would give you a desire to pursue wisdom.
2. Proverbs 16:16 tells us, "How much better to get wisdom than gold! To get understanding is to be chosen rather than silver." Do you believe that it's better to seek wisdom than wealth? If so, how do

you prioritize the pursuit of wisdom over the goal of making money?

3. Grab a friend and tell them about the challenge to read a chapter of Proverbs and Matthew a day. Invite them to participate alongside you. Pray that God would bring you insights together that you likely wouldn't have discovered on your own.

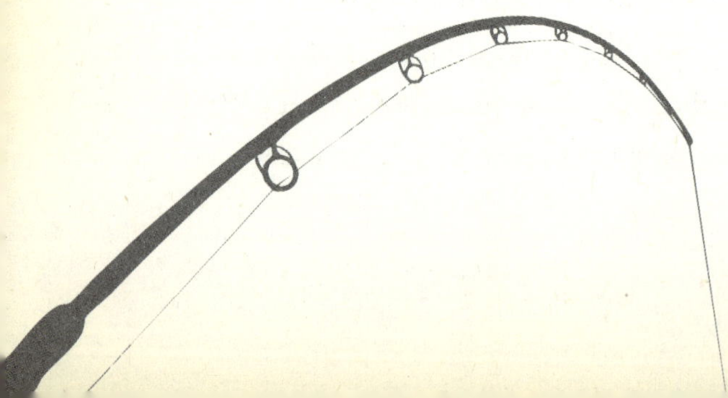

32

YOU'RE IN THE STORY

The sport demands immersion, from air to water, from warm blood to cold, to a view of the racing universe and all its stars through a river's flowing lens.

Thomas McGuane, *The Longest Silence*

Scripture to Read: Psalm 119:105–112; 2 Peter 1:19–21

We'd just finished a great morning of fishing on Lake Bemidji. The summer after I graduated from high school, a friend invited me to fish with him and his father in Minnesota. His dad was a good fisherman. The first morning, he taught us how to read elevation maps, looking for where the deeper flats transition from hard bottom to soft. We caught several walleye, northern pike, and yellow perch. My friend's dad even had a muskie follow his lure up to the boat.

I'd just landed my best fish of the morning, a twenty-four-inch walleye, when we heard another boat's engine getting closer. We were in a no-wake area, but the oncoming craft was running full throttle, sending swells behind it in both directions. They were coming straight toward us. I could hear their voices; they were laughing and talking loudly without knowing we were there.

My friend's dad yelled to get their attention, and when that didn't work, he grabbed an air horn and sounded the deafening alarm. The driver of the other boat, who had been turned around to face his friends, spun on a dime and killed the throttle, creating another swell, this one headed straight out from the bow.

Our boats settled within a few feet of each other, close enough that we didn't need to yell to talk. Arguably, yelling would have been understandable, but my friend's father restrained himself. He was calm as he asked the boys if they were all right.

"I'm really sorry, sir," the young man behind the wheel of the other boat said. "I just got this boat. To be honest, I have no idea what I'm doing yet."

Our boats had now drifted to the point that I needed to reach out and put pressure on the hull of their craft so we didn't hit each other. I could see the faces of all four passengers. They were ashen, not all that dissimilar from the soft, plastic, grayish-yellow swimbaits we'd been throwing for northern pike. These guys were shaken up.

My friend's dad reached into a small plastic tote and pulled out a copy of *Minnesota Boating Guide*. He held it up for the driver to see. "Son, have you seen one of these before?"

The young man shook his head.

My friend's dad handed it to him. "I'd suggest you read every word before you go an inch further."

The boy declared he would. We wished one another well and separated our boats.

As the *Minnesota Boating Guide* intends to help drivers learn how to operate a boat, the truths and doctrines in the Bible teach us everything we need to know about walking with God.

In his book *The Drama of Doctrine*, Kevin Vanhoozer likens the Bible to the script of a play. The script is essential; without it, the cast would have no idea how to act out their parts. The script unifies the entire cast and helps them move in the same direction. Vanhoozer writes, "The purpose of doctrine is to ensure that those who bear Christ's name walk in Christ's way."[29]

Life is complex and surprising. Sometimes, you go out on the water for what you expect to be a relaxing time, and another boat almost runs you over. We're shocked by one thing after another, and many of today's challenges aren't mentioned in the Bible. Boats didn't go sixty miles an hour in biblical times. The New Testament world hadn't encountered cyberterrorism, online dating, or the depression caused by social media. The fact that the Scriptures don't mention many of our modern issues leads some to think that the Bible isn't relevant.

That idea is false. What Paul wrote in the first century is just as relevant and practical for our lives in the twenty-first century. In 2 Timothy 3:16–17, he writes, "All Scripture is breathed out by God and profitable for teaching, for reproof, for correction, and for training in righteousness, that the man of God may be complete, equipped for every good work."

While it's true that the Bible doesn't directly address many of our specific situations today, it is still our script. When a Christian knows and trusts the Scriptures, the Holy Spirit takes the truths and story of the Bible and directs us in how to think, feel, speak, and act in a biblically faithful manner. Indeed, Christians living out the script together is one of the ways the Lord illustrates the story of the Bible in every age.

As I write this devotion, I'm listening to Yo-Yo Ma perform Bach's "Cello Suite No. 1." How Ma plays the notes Bach put on paper is an excellent example of the way we are to perform the truths of the Bible. As Ma turns Bach's ink into an event in time, the body of Christ shows the world the story told in the pages of our Holy Scriptures.

Doctrine matters. Knowing the Bible matters. Living it out the best we can by the power of God's Spirit matters. Let us not move forward another inch without reading the Book.

QUESTIONS FOR FURTHER REFLECTION:

1. In the previous devotion, I challenged you to read a chapter from Proverbs and Matthew's gospel each day for a month. Following that challenge, what could be your plan to continue to engage God's Word in an intentional manner each day?
2. Are there sections of the Bible that you feel less familiar with? Consider reading them next.
3. Describe a time when the Spirit of God helped you improvise—to apply the script—during a challenge not specifically addressed in the Bible.

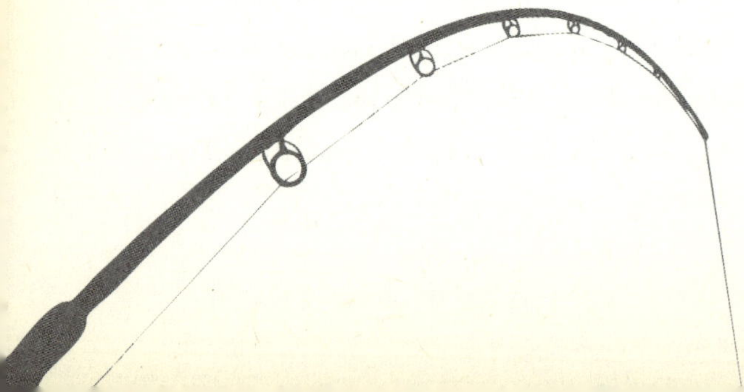

33

PREPARE TO BE SHOCKED

It is too much like a fisherman's tale. One of the remarkable things about fishermen is that they never really expected to catch anything. They go out loaded with tackle, but they always knew the fish wouldn't bite.

E. T. Brown, *Not without Prejudice: Essays on Assorted Subjects*

Scripture to Read: John 11:1–53; James 4:13–17

Jay Yelas has hooked thousands of fish during his thirty-plus years as a professional angler, but there's only one he calls his "most dramatic catch ever."

It happened on day two of the 2002 Bassmaster Classic. Jay was fishing the Coosa River near the Logan Martin Dam. The Army Corps of Engineers controlled the flows in this narrow waterway. The lake was too shallow in the morning for boat travel, but the corps increased the output in the afternoon, and the depth rose to about five feet. Jay had figured out that large fish swam toward the dam along the bank when the flows increased.

Jay was atop the leaderboard, and about forty spectator boats packed the area with enthusiastic fans watching him fish those headwaters. There was another boat on the water that afternoon, one that wasn't connected to the tournament and, it's safe to say, wasn't carrying any Jay Yelas fans. Perhaps it was a group of locals who knew that area, knew about the large fish that followed the flows, and had hoped to have them to themselves that day. Whatever their story, they opened the throttle and charged straight toward Jay's boat.

The driver of the large pontoon boat swerved away just a few feet before making contact but kept the engine open as he plowed along the bank, the precise spot Jay was about to fish. The spectators gasped. Swells smacked the side of Jay's boat.

Jay is one of the fishermen I admire most in the world—and the one I asked to write the afterword for this book—mainly because he is kind and generous. He has a warm personality that springs from his love for Jesus. His reaction to this encounter is a great example.

Life with God is not a formula; it is not predictable. This calls us to be humble about the future.

An ESPN cameraman on Jay's boat recorded this entire moment; if you watch it, you'll see that Jay's response displayed shock and playfulness, exasperation and laughter. It also displayed a realistic expectation for his next cast. You can still hear the pontoon boat racing away when Jay turns to the cameraman and says, "It'll take an act of God to make one bite in there now."

Still in shock, Jay cast, slinging his lure into the water that the prop had turned to sludge.

He got a hit. He set the hook.

The strike was so strong that if you listen closely to the video, you can hear Jay whisper, "What is this? It can't be a bass."

It was a bass. It was the largest bass of the entire tournament, weighing in at six pounds thirteen ounces.

This moment illustrates an essential reality of the Christian life: we follow a God who surprises us. D. A. Carson rightly states:

> This is not because He is whimsical or arbitrary or bad-tempered. He is always entirely consistent with his own character. But his wisdom and his knowledge are so vastly incomparable to ours that he does all kinds of things we wouldn't have predicted and certainly do not foresee.[30]

The Bible gives us many stories of people shocked because God did something they didn't expect. Consider Moses as a young man, when he killed an Egyptian fighting against an Israelite, believing he was about to lead a revolution to free God's people. It had to be quite shocking for him when God planted him in a desert for the next forty years—before surprising him once again by calling him out of retirement. He was eighty when God freed Israel from Egypt's slavery under Moses's leadership.

Picture the shock on the faces of the cowering, fearful Israelite army when David, perhaps only fourteen or fifteen at the time, faced

Goliath in an open field. Then, imagine their astonishment when the teenager dropped the Philistine behemoth with a single rock.

Review in your mind how the disciples scattered in fear and disbelief after the One they'd come to believe was the Messiah died on a Roman cross. Recall the shock of the women who went to the tomb to anoint Jesus' dead body, only to find the tomb empty. Consider the passage we read today (John 11) and the amazement of Lazarus's family when, after he had died and had been decomposing for four days, Jesus spoke into the tomb, "Lazarus, come out!" ... and he came.

It's all surprising. It's all quite shocking.

These moments in the biblical narrative, together with our own moments of being surprised by God, remind us that things aren't necessarily as they seem, *precisely because God is God*. They help us see that life with God is not a formula; it is not predictable. This calls us to be humble about the future, as James commands:

> Come now, you who say, "Today or tomorrow we will go into such and such a town and spend a year there and trade and make a profit"—yet you do not know what tomorrow will bring. What is your life? For you are a mist that appears for a little time and then vanishes. Instead you ought to say, "If the Lord wills, we will live and do this or that." (James 4:13–15)

It's important to remember that when God surprises us—positively or negatively—He's giving us the gift of showing us His glory. In John 11, before Jesus brought Lazarus back to life, He made a key statement to Martha (and all of us). The crowd approached the tomb, and Jesus said, "Take away the stone" (v. 39a).

Looking at the facts of the situation, Martha, Lazarus's sister, replied, "Lord, by this time there will be an odor, for he has been dead four days" (v. 39b).

Jesus replied, "Did I not tell you that if you believed you would see the glory of God?" (v. 40b).

The first part of that statement makes it clear what our role is in our relationship with Jesus: We are to believe Him. We are to trust in a God who has plans and carries them out, even if they seem unlikely to us. We live by faith in Jesus, not in our best assessments of the situation before us.

In the second part of the statement, Jesus told Martha that if she lived by faith in a God who is in control and does whatever He wants in heaven and on earth, she would see the glory of God. She and all those who share her faith will have eyes to see the beauties, powers, and works of God around them.

When I talked with Jay about that "most dramatic catch," it was clear that he had seen the glory of God. When he'd said it would take an act of God to make a fish bite after the pontoon boat had sped through, he wasn't testing God. He wasn't asking God for a tournament win. He wasn't working an incantation that required him to invoke God's name. In shock, he'd simply blurted out the obvious—that, apart from a surprise from God, that spot was ruined.

On that day, God chose to surprise Jay (and thousands of people like me who were watching on ESPN) with an incredible moment. Jay described it to me like this: "For some surprising reason known only to God Himself, He made it happen. It was a beautiful, faith-inspiring moment. How could I not give God all the glory for the championship after all He had done?"

QUESTIONS FOR FURTHER REFLECTION:

1. How has God surprised you recently? Was it a positive or negative surprise?
2. How did the situation help you see God's beauties, glory, and works in your life or other people's lives? Did that moment bring about a proper humility in your heart?
3. Why do you think we struggle with the idea that God isn't predictable?

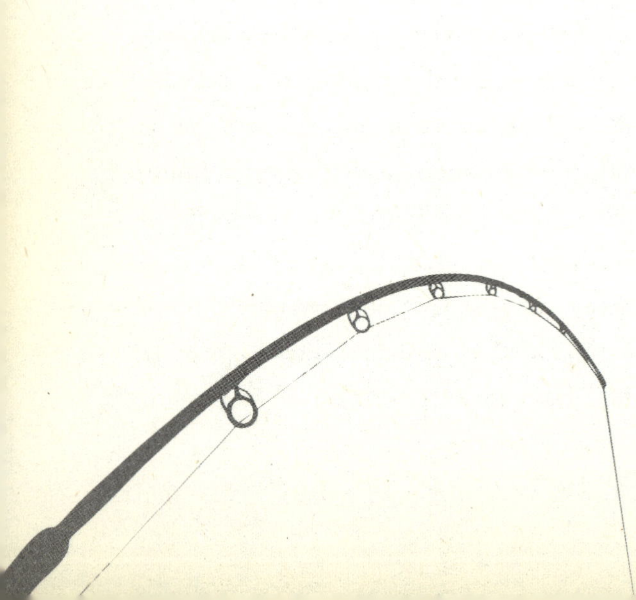

34

RHYTHMS

As for my father, I never knew whether he believed God was a mathematician, but he certainly believed God could count and that only by picking up God's rhythms were we able to regain power and beauty.

Norman Maclean, *A River Runs through It*

Scripture to Read: Ecclesiastes 3:1–13; Hebrews 4:1–16

My friend Rob and I recently took our other friend Steve to our favorite river. Rob and I had been throwing flies into this waterway for years, but Steve was new to the area and new to fly fishing. We knew he'd figure things out quickly; Steve's a researcher at heart and a quick study of anything he sets his mind to. In the weeks before our trip, Steve had studied insect hatches, river currents, and trout behavior. On the drive out, he shared his findings with Rob and me, and we learned some things.

It was early spring, and the trout only had eyes for worms, scuds, and midges. Rob and I rigged Steve's line with the same flies we were throwing, and then the three of us spread out just far enough so that our lines wouldn't cross. The fish were hungry from winter, and the bite was on. Within a few minutes, Rob hooked into a nice one. I walked upstream and slipped my net under a bright-pink rainbow. Netting a friend's fish is one of the purest joys in the world.

For humanity to flourish, we must pause from our efforts and be satisfied by the person and work of God.

Rob and I landed several trout in the first couple of hours. With each fish, our hopes grew for Steve to join us in the excitement. He didn't, though, so I hooked my fly to an eyelet, reeled in my line, and walked over to investigate. I checked his system. His flies were attached and still had hooks. The weight and indicator were in the right places. His rig seemed fine.

"Mind if I step back and watch you cast a few times?" I asked. He welcomed the offer.

Watching Steve, I saw the problem right away. He was doing a lot of things right. He cast upstream at the correct angle and into the proper seam of the river. His form and aim were great. Yet while his line and indicator drifted in the current, Steve, always the researcher, examined everything around him. He watched a flock of geese land upriver. He studied the insects that landed on his arms. During one drift, he took out his phone and snapped pictures of an antelope on the hill across from us.

As Steve watched the environment, I watched his indicator. He got multiple strikes. I saw them. He didn't.

Steve was used to bass fishing. When you're retrieving a spinner or crankbait, you can watch geese or turn to talk with your friends. When a bass slams your line, you know it, whether you're looking or not. Fly fishing is different. Trout rarely grab your fly. They typically nose up to it, open their jaws, and let the inflow of water pull your fly into the front of their mouths. A trout's brain is roughly the size of a pea, but if you spend a day fly fishing, you'll think they're smarter than Einstein. It takes these fish a mere fraction of a second to sense your fly is fake and eject it back into the current.

To hook one of these wary creatures, you must watch every tiny movement your indicator makes. If it ducks under the surface or darts to the side a quarter of an inch, you'd better see it and respond, or the now-even-wiser trout will push away from the dinner table and retreat to the depths until he thinks you're gone.

We either work too hard without breaks or rest too often without being productive. Both workaholism and laziness keep the human heart discontented, never feeling productive, satisfied, or at peace.

There are rhythms to a trout river. It changes day by day, season by season. The rhythm of any one spot can change several times a day because of insect hatches, water generation schedules, or weather systems. There are also rhythms to fly fishing—to casting, mending line, and setting the hook when a wise old trout ever so slightly sucks your fly into its mouth. While the rhythms of rivers, trout, and fishing are impossible to master, a thoughtful angler can study and sync up with them.

For this reason, fly fishing is an ideal metaphor for the Christian life. God is a God of order, not chaos. There is a cadence to how God created all things. Each of the first six days of His creative work comes to an end with the statement, "And there was evening and there was morning." Consider the first day as an example: "God called the light Day, and the darkness he called Night. And there was evening and there was morning, the first day" (Gen. 1:5).

This pattern shows us not only the way God created all things but also the very nature of His creation. God designed this world to be well-ordered and governed by seasons, as Solomon described in Ecclesiastes:

> For everything there is a season, and a time for every
> matter under heaven:
> a time to be born, and a time to die;
> a time to plant, and a time to pluck up what is
> planted;
> a time to kill, and a time to heal. (3:1–3a)

It is essential to notice that the seventh day of creation doesn't have this evening-morning formula. This day is different from the first six, showing us another aspect of the nature of God's creation: God rested on the seventh day. And His rest didn't have an end—implying that He still enjoys His rest today. The seventh day shows us that life isn't merely about work, cultivation, and production. It's also about rest and satisfaction. For humanity to flourish, we must pause from our efforts and be satisfied by the person and work of God.

The idea of Sabbath—of human beings setting down their work to rest and trust in God—was so important that God set this rhythm into the weekly life of Israel. The third commandment He gave Moses states, "Remember the Sabbath day, to keep it holy" (Ex. 20:8).

The God who turned a chaotic earth into a vibrant garden changes sinners into new creations.

The Israelites in the Old Testament represent all of us as they struggled to live in the work-rest patterns God created. We either work too hard without breaks or rest too often without being productive. Both workaholism and laziness keep the human heart discontented, never feeling productive, satisfied, or at peace.

This is one of many reasons we need Jesus. God sent Jesus to give us perfect work and perfect rest. The Gospels show us how, as God rested after His work of creation, Jesus rested after His work of making all things new. Jesus perfectly fulfilled the law and then died on the cross to become the final payment for our sins. This was the work the Father gave the Son, and Jesus did it perfectly. At the end of His work, Jesus entered His rest—the satisfaction and joy of knowing the work was finished. Nothing more will ever be needed. As Jesus said on the cross immediately before giving up His spirit, "It is finished" (John 19:30b).

We enter Jesus' rest by trusting in His completed work, as the author of Hebrews writes, "We who have believed enter that rest" (4:3a).

Like the rhythms of fly fishing, there are rhythms to life with God. We'll never master them, but we can study and sync up with them. The God who turned a chaotic earth into a vibrant garden changes sinners into new creations (see 2 Cor. 5:17). By grace, we can love His ways and walk wisely through the seasons He gives.

Steve's fly-fishing problem had an easy fix. He simply had to stay attuned to his line and indicator, then set the hook the instant he saw movement. It took him a couple of casts to find his rhythm, and then he outfished Rob and me for the rest of the day.

QUESTIONS FOR FURTHER REFLECTION:

1. Do you tend toward workaholism? Do you struggle to take off because you feel everything rests on your shoulders? If so, ask God to help you see that He, not you, sustains all things.
2. Do you tend toward laziness? Do you have a hard time delighting in rest because you haven't worked hard the rest of the week? If so, ask God to help you see that the work He's given to you matters.
3. What are ways that you can more wisely live in the work and rest God intends for us as people? How does the finished work and perfect, eternal rest of Christ enable you to sync up with the rhythms of God?

35

UGLY DISTRACTS FROM BEAUTY

The rest of his conversation was swallowed by river sounds, for it is so noisy in those rips that you can smile at a partner, call him a no-good stiff and he will actually think you are complimenting him.

Gordon MacQuarrie, *The Gordon MacQuarrie Sporting Treasury*

Scripture to Read: Colossians 3:12–14; 1 John 2:1–6

It's by the grace of God that I didn't get myself into boiling hot water. A church in Wyoming booked me to speak at their annual anglers' event. The evening was designed to be an outreach into the greater community. When the event organizer, Ted, called me to inquire if I was available, he mentioned that he was organizing the event because he loves sharing the gospel with non-Christians. I was an easy sell. I enjoy speaking at hunting and fishing gatherings, and the North Platte is one of my favorite places to fly fish.

I drove to the area the night before the event to fish for a few hours before heading to the church. About midmorning the next day, I hiked through sagebrush to a bend in the river I knew was packed with fish.

Two fishermen were in the spot, so I dropped into the water about a hundred yards upstream. An hour later, I noticed the anglers were gone, so I walked down and waded out to the sweet spot. I hooked a nice trout on my first cast.

As I released the fish, I heard, "Hey, we were fishing this spot. We'd like it back!"

I turned to see the two anglers I'd seen earlier. They were about twenty feet behind me. The one who had just spoken took off his sunglasses. I could see in his eyes that he wasn't asking; he was telling.

I'm not proud to admit it, but some snide comments flashed through my mind as potential responses. This isn't how things work on the river. If you vacate a spot for thirty minutes, it's open. I'm also not proud to confess that I don't always bite my tongue and restrain my words. But this time, thankfully, I remained silent. I thought it over and decided I wasn't particularly interested in getting into a scuffle. Leaving aside Jason Bourne and John Wick, one person doesn't often fare well against two, so I hooked my fly on an eyelet and said, "It's all yours, guys."

I walked back upstream and fished my original spot for another hour before calling it quits.

Two hours later, I pulled into the parking lot of the church. I grabbed my Bible and a box of books and walked through the front doors. Ted, the event organizer I'd spoken with over the phone a few months earlier, was waiting. He crossed the foyer and extended his hand, saying, "Zeke, it's great to have you!"

I grabbed his hand and looked into the eyes of the man who'd told me he loves sharing the gospel. They were the same eyes I had seen in that encounter on the river two hours earlier.

The realization struck Ted at precisely the same instant it hit me. His face turned red, a shade not unlike the one you'd find on the jaws of a Yellowstone cutthroat. The awkwardness of that moment in the foyer dwarfed the unpleasantness of the one on the water.

We Christians can care deeply about the gospel yet allow the ugliness of our flesh to hurt our witness. This isn't new. Some Christians in the New Testament had bad moments as well. I admit to taking a bit of comfort in the fact that even those who walked with Jesus didn't always act like Him. For example, Paul rebuked Peter (aka Cephas) for not acting in accordance with the gospel he'd been preaching: "When Cephas came to Antioch, I opposed him to his face, because he stood condemned" (Gal. 2:11).

Yet the fact that even the apostles sometimes failed to act like Jesus while presenting the gospel doesn't permit us to do the same. Certainly, our growth in Christlikeness should be a movement toward the place where our practiced beliefs align with our stated ones. If we proclaim a tenderhearted Savior who was willing to give up His life to serve others, we should seek to model His compassionate, kind ways as we speak His truth. It's not enough to present Christ. We must also strive to embody Jesus.

The apostle Paul instructed Titus that those who *teach* what is good are to *do* what is good. If you communicate the gospel, Paul writes, you must "show yourself in all respects to be a model of good works, and in your teaching show integrity, dignity, and sound speech that cannot be condemned, so that an opponent may be put to shame, having nothing evil to say about us" (Titus 2:7–8).

Thankfully, no one else was in the foyer during that moment between Ted and me. We moved to a couple of chairs along the wall and waded into the afternoon's events. Ted was genuinely humble, displaying the brokenness I assume Peter experienced when he received Paul's rebuke. Only I didn't have to say a word to Ted; the Spirit of God was at work in the heart of my brother in Christ. Ted cried as he asked for forgiveness. I cried as I granted it. I told him it was easy to forgive him because I'd done similar things. I've shown people the uglies of Zeke instead of the beauties of Christ.

Within a few moments, Ted and I were celebrating God's mercy and patience. We prayed together, and then we served Christ together. What we'd gone through in the afternoon primed our hearts to celebrate the gospel with hundreds of anglers at the event that evening.

At the end of the night, Ted walked me to my truck. We hugged and said goodbye, but not before declaring our hopes of fishing that spot together sometime soon.

QUESTIONS FOR FURTHER REFLECTION:

1. Is there any area of your life that comes to mind where what you do doesn't align with what you teach or say you believe? I encourage you to confess this to the Lord and a friend.
2. What steps do you need to take to bring your practiced theology and your stated theology into alignment?
3. How does knowing you've received God's grace and mercy enable you to more quickly give grace and mercy to those who sin against you?

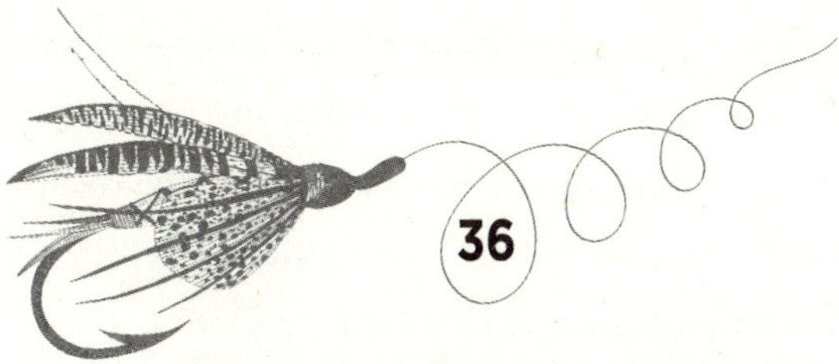

36

WAITING WELL

Perhaps the most difficult labor for my species is to accept its limits, its weakness and ignorance. But here I am.

Wendell Berry, "*An Entrance to the Woods*"

Scripture to Read: Matthew 24:36–25:46

There are two options, and both can lead to strange conversations. I occasionally hire an outfitter to help me figure out a new river. The poor unsuspecting guide has no idea he's about to spend an entire day trapped in a boat with a pastor, a frightening factoid that invariably emerges in the early moments of an outing.

My first option is to wait and let the guide ask what I do for a living. The awkwardness of that scenario stems from the fact that by that point we've already spent a good amount of time together—time in which the guide has often told crass jokes or dropped a barrage of four-letter words. I've watched more than a few guides replay the previous moments in their heads to make sure they've apologized for everything they'd just said to a minister. I always assure them they didn't offend me, explaining how I'm a real person and that I want them to be themselves. That usually relieves some of the awkwardness but never wholly removes it.

My other option—telling the guide in advance—can also make things strange. This happened recently when my pastoral colleague Travis joined me on a fishing trip in southern Missouri. My heart especially went out to this outfitter. James had to spend an entire day in the boat with not one but two men of the cloth.

James called me the night before our trip to arrange a meeting time and place. I rolled the dice and opted for the second option, mentioning to him that he'd be spending time with two fish-bum pastors the next day. In hindsight, I gave our guide too much time with that information. As soon as we launched the boat, James began sharing his religious questions and theories. And he had a full day's worth, most of them pertaining to end-time events.

How we wait for Jesus is a serious matter. We must spend our time on earth treating one another as Christ treats us.

"Do you think what's happening between Israel and Palestine is signaling that the Lord is returning soon?"

"Do you think so-and-so could be the Antichrist?"

"When do you think Jesus will return? I read one book that said it would be after the next election and another that said it could be another two thousand years."

Most of James's questions were impossible to answer definitively from the Bible. I admitted to him that the more I study apocalyptic literature—books like Daniel and Revelation—the humbler I become about the details surrounding Jesus' return. What seems clear, I suggested, is that how we wait for Jesus' return should be our primary focus.

In Matthew 24:36–25:46, Jesus gives us five parables, each adding details about how Jesus wants us to wait for His return. Let's consider these five parables briefly.

Parable 1 (24:36–44): Jesus refers to Noah and the ark to encourage us to prepare for that day by obeying His words. Noah diligently followed the words of God while others were "eating and drinking, marrying and giving in marriage, until the day when Noah entered the ark" (24:38b). Not that it's wrong to eat, drink, or get married today. As we've previously discussed, God determines the plans and purposes of each season, and this waiting period is missional. We must not get distracted by the cares and pleasures of this world.

Parable 2 (24:45–51): Jesus describes a faithful servant in contrast to a wicked servant. He's encouraging us to wait as people who know we will give an account of how we treat others. We must not do cruel and selfish things because we've foolishly forgotten that Jesus sees everything and is returning to set everything right.

Parable 3 (25:1–13): Jesus describes five foolish bridesmaids in contrast to five wise ones. The wise virgins showed their wisdom in preparing to wait an undefined amount of time for their friend's bridegroom. They took extra oil and trimmed their wicks, which proved they would be ready whenever that moment came. We must not see Jesus' delay as evidence that He's not coming. He is!

Parable 4 (25:14–30): Jesus gives the parable of a master who, before leaving, gives his servants various sums of money (an amount referred to as a talent). Jesus entrusted the riches of the gospel to us to invest in people. The gospel is a precious treasure, and we must maximize our impact by sharing Christ every chance we get. We shouldn't spend our time building our empires. This waiting period is our chance to invest our lives in Jesus' kingdom.

Parable 5 (25:31–46): Jesus describes His return and the judgment that will immediately ensue. Jesus sees everything that happens today with perfect clarity and will judge it with absolute equity. There will be a separation of the sheep and goats. The sheep, those who loved others as Christ loved them, will enter the kingdom of God. The goats, those who didn't walk in a manner worthy of their calling, will be cast into "the eternal fire prepared for the devil and his angels" (v. 41b). If this feels sobering, it's because it is. How we wait for Jesus is a serious matter. We must spend our time on earth treating one another as Christ treats us.

Each time James brought up his end-time questions or theories, I returned to this whole passage and the importance of waiting well. I tried to sound more like a trout bum who loves Jesus than a preacher using the boat's bow as a pulpit.

As we trailered the boat, James said, "So, you're saying it's not about cracking codes. It's about knowing that day is coming and being ready?"

"I couldn't have said it better," I replied.

And indeed, I couldn't have. My words on the boat that day seemed clumsy compared to his elegant conclusion of the matter.

QUESTIONS FOR FURTHER REFLECTION:

1. Are you more interested in how Christ will return or how you're investing your time and treasure in light of this inevitable event?
2. Which of the five parables we read in Matthew's gospel most convicts and challenges you about the way you're waiting for Jesus' return? What changes do you need to make to wait well?
3. What are ways that you can remind yourself each day to wait with urgency for the return of Jesus?

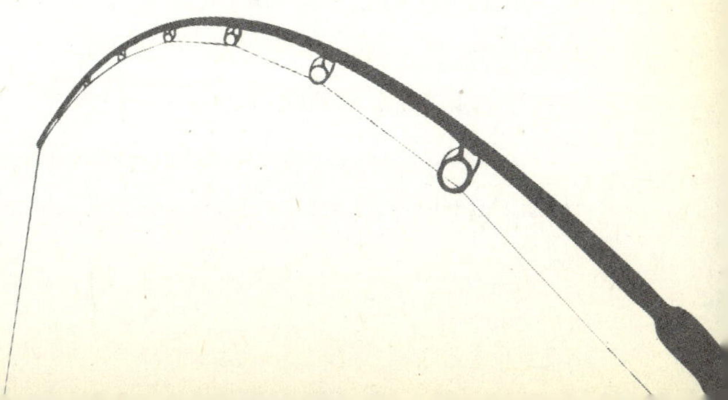

37

HOW WE TREAT FISH

But all the things that God would have us do are hard for us to do—remember that—and hence, he oftener commands us than endeavours to persuade. And if we obey God, we must disobey ourselves; and it is in this disobeying ourselves, wherein the hardness of obeying God consists.

Herman Melville, *Moby-Dick*

Scripture to Read: Psalm 19:1–14; Romans 6:15–23

It's one of the most profound statements I've ever heard a parent make. My then-three-year-old daughter Kate and I were fishing for bluegill in a public park in Ames, Iowa. A father and his son, perhaps eight years old, fished a few feet from us. Like Kate, the boy had lost interest in fishing. While Kate was picking flowers, the boy played with a bluegill he'd pulled from his father's stringer. He poked it in the eye with a rock, then started putting gravel chips into the fish's mouth. When the fish dried out, the boy stuck it to the underside of his hand and held it up.

"Look, Dad, it sticks to me like glue!"

The dad looked, and I'll never forget what he said to his son. "Stop that! Put the fish back in the water. What you're doing is hurtful."

"It's okay, Dad," the son replied. "My teacher told us that fish don't feel pain."

The dad paused and then said, "It's not the fish I'm worried about, Son."

Proverbs 16:17 says, "The highway of the upright turns aside from evil; whoever guards his way preserves his life." The word *preserves* means "to keep or protect." Behind the English word *life* in this verse is the Hebrew word *nephesh*, which refers to our inner lives: our thoughts, feelings, and desires. Our inner life is the epicenter of our character, and Proverbs teaches us that this arena is not static. It's always in motion. It's either growing in spiritual health or being formed toward selfishness and chaos.

What determines whether our character develops into godliness and life or sinfulness and death?

The decisions we make. Our choices every day, on significant issues and small ones alike.

When we choose to do the right thing, the biblically ethical thing, whether anyone else is watching or not, we form our character toward godliness and spiritual health. When we decide to lie, leave income off our tax filing, or poke a fish in the eye because someone told us they don't feel pain, we form our character toward cruelty and callousness.

The issue here, as we discussed in the previous devotion, is related to how we wait for Jesus' return. We wait well when we seek to be transformed into the likeness of Christ. Jesus' death, burial, and resurrection give us a new way to live *today*. Our salvation isn't merely a ticket into heaven that we punch when we die. It's an opportunity right now, right here, to be "built up as a spiritual house, to be a holy priesthood, to offer spiritual sacrifices acceptable to God through Jesus Christ" (1 Pet. 2:5b).

This vision for making choices according to the will of God and the imminent return of Jesus confronts a widespread belief in our society that says, "You should be driven by your commitment to yourself." Our culture believes that "being true to yourself" is the highest possible good. We use rhetorically powerful terms and phrases like "authenticity" and "live your truth" to encourage one another to do whatever feels right or comes naturally. We celebrate self-creation and call those who do whatever they want "courageous."

These ideas sound good. They fall upon our ears like honey dripping onto our tongues. Many of us grew up saturated in this ideology. To the extent that we've believed it, we've formed our inner lives not only to want but even to demand whatever feels right to us. But this philosophy comes from the pit of hell, and practicing it has created a generation more depressed and anxious than any previous one.

It's also redirected people from the joys of following Christ. Doing what we want or what comes naturally to us turns us from the path of life. Jesus teaches us that we find our spiritual health when we deny ourselves, take up our cross, and follow Him (see Matt. 16:24). Killing the self, not promoting it, leads to joy. Obeying God's truth, not ours, leads to life.

It's important to remember that the Spirit of God transforms our hearts. Our role is to have faith in Jesus and trust Him so sincerely that we make the right choices each day. We choose godliness because Jesus made us holy. Herman Bavinck writes,

> The good tree comes before the good fruits. We do not live through good works but for them; we fulfill

> the law not for eternal life but out of it, for this life has been planted in our hearts through faith. It is according to this order alone that a true moral life is possible.[31]

The boy with the bluegill glued to his hand was noticeably confused by his father's comment. The dad sat beside his son, put his arm around him, and began to explain. Watching the moment unfold, I thought of something George Herbert wrote: "One father is more than a hundred schoolmasters."[32]

I would have loved to stay and listen, but I grabbed our stringer of fish and directed Kate to the car. She had enough flowers in her hand, and I had plenty of fish for dinner. More than that, it seemed like a holy moment. Like Moses' sandals when Moses stood before the burning bush, Kate and I needed to be removed.

QUESTIONS FOR FURTHER REFLECTION:

1. Can you think of a decision you've made recently that moved you toward godly character and life or toward callousness and self-centeredness? Describe it.
2. Can you think of someone who is faithful and godly? Let me challenge you to ask them how they developed that character throughout their life.
3. Are there "little" sins you're committing because you think they won't have an impact on your spiritual formation? If so, what is your plan now?

38

BROOK TROUT

Is it fair to say that country is more real than ours?
That its stone is harder, its water more drenching—that
the weather itself is alert and not just background?
Can you endure a witness to its tactile presence?

Leif Enger, *Peace like a River*

Scripture to Read: Psalm 34:4–5; Matthew 4:17–25

The most beautiful fish I've ever held was a ten-inch brook trout from the gin-clear waters of Indian Peaks Wilderness in Colorado. I know that any purist reading this might wish to remind me that brookies aren't trout; they're char. I grant that. We can debate what to call them. What I'm sure of is that, with their gorgeous blue and red spots rising from their sunset-colored bellies, there's not a trout alive that wouldn't welcome this char into the family. A brook trout hovering behind a freestone boulder symbolizes radiance, life, and possibility.

This is how Cormac McCarthy used brook trout in his novel *The Road*. The book tells the story of a father and son's journey toward the coast after some apocalyptic event obliterated the earth. It's one of my favorite books—but I'll warn you: it's bleak. Most of humanity has died, and the few survivors the father and son encounter are cruel and vile. Ash covers everything, making the reader wonder if hope exists for the future. There is hope, and McCarthy gives it to us in the final paragraph of the book:

> Once there were brook trout in the streams in the mountains. You could see them standing in the amber current where the white edges of their fins wimpled softly in the flow. They smelled of moss in your hand. Polished and muscular and torsional. On their backs were vermiculate patterns that were maps of the world in its becoming. Maps and mazes. Of a thing which could not be put back. Not be made right again. In the deep glens where they lived all things were older than man and they hummed of mystery.[33]

This passage signals timelessness. It takes us into the past yet also foreshadows a future renewal. McCarthy's precise meaning behind this shocking final paragraph is the subject of great debate. It seems he was purposefully ambiguous. He ends the book with the word "mystery," which seems an obvious tell. For whatever reason, McCarthy used the smell, color, and "vermiculate patterns" of brook trout as metaphors for life, vibrancy, and health. He ends the novel with a symbol of hope: a fish in a river.

God ends His Book in a similar manner. He describes a river to give us hope for our future life. In Revelation 22, John writes, "Then the angel showed me the river of the water of life, bright as crystal, flowing from the throne of God and of the Lamb through the middle of the street of the city; also, on either side of the river, the tree of life with its twelve kinds of fruit, yielding its fruit each month" (vv. 1–2b).

The One from whose side blood and water flowed at the cross is the One who will supply us throughout all eternity with living water.

As discussed in chapter 12, water symbolizes the gift of life that God alone gives. Remember the four rivers in the garden of Eden, Hagar and Ishmael's well in the wilderness, and the fountain flowing from rocks as Israel journeyed to the Promised Land? Where God provides water, He gives life. Where He gives life, creation flourishes. This is why the "tree of life" (v. 2), which is fed directly by the "river of the water of life" (v. 1), yields "twelve kinds of fruit, yielding its fruit each month" (v. 2).

Twelve is symbolic of a complete, perfect amount. The Tree of Life will nourish and revitalize all of God's creation. That the Tree of Life bears its fruit each month shows us that it never takes a break, never stops producing. Because the river of life supplies the Tree of Life, our eternity with God will be unending joy and satisfaction.

But what is the river of the water of life? Looking beyond the symbol, what are we to find?

Who are we to find? is the better question. Notice in Revelation 22:1 how the river of life flows directly from the throne of God. It doesn't originate beside, below, or above the throne of God. It's not springing from the ground immediately in front of the throne of God. John tells us that the river is sourced directly *from the throne*. God is the source of the river of life, which means that the pleasures of being with Him will never run out. There will be no more loss, pain, suffering, drought, or starvation in the new heavens and new earth. There will be no more sin and death, precisely because the river of life flows directly from God. His supply of life and joy are infinite and unending.

What ensures that sinful people like you and me will reach heaven?

What makes it sure that we will remain there for all eternity?

What guarantees that we will enjoy a vibrancy of life there unlike any we've ever known here?

The fact that the river at the end of God's Book flows "from the throne of God and of the Lamb" (Rev. 22:1b). Jesus, our Savior, who promised "whoever drinks of the water that I will give him will never be thirsty again" (John 4:14a), is our source of life. The One from whose side blood and water flowed at the cross is the One who will supply us throughout all eternity with living water, "bright as crystal" (Rev. 22:1b).

Let the river and fish before your eyes remind you that Jesus overcame this world with all its troubles. In Him, all our thirsts will one day be quenched.

This life is hard. It's filled with trouble. My friend, the next time you encounter a dry, barren, seemingly hopeless season, remember the river of life. If it's hard to picture, consider visiting one of the many pristine streams and rivers around the world that are home to brook trout. You don't even need to fish. Just sit beside the water. Watch the grace in their movements, and behold the artistry in the "vermiculate patterns" on their backs. Their "maps and mazes," as McCarthy describes them.

Let the river and fish before your eyes remind you that Jesus overcame this world with all its troubles. In Him, all our thirsts will one day be quenched. "In the world you will have tribulation. But take heart; I have overcome the world" (John 16:33b).

QUESTIONS FOR FURTHER REFLECTION:

1. Do you look forward to the new heavens and the new earth? If so, what difficulties in your life encourage you to long for the resurrected life to come?
2. Does water hold the power to encourage you and refresh your heart? Let me offer you this challenge: the next time you feel that way, give thanks to God for His provision.
3. What are some of the pains and hardships you're experiencing today that you will be glad to have redeemed and restored in the new heavens and new earth?

39

IT'S ALL A GIFT

Something will have gone out of us as a people if we ever let the remaining wilderness be destroyed.... We simply need that wild country available to us, even if we never do more than drive to its edge and look in.

Wallace Stegner, "*The Wilderness Letter*"

Scripture to Read: Jeremiah 10:11–16; Romans 1:18–25

"I feel so close to God when I'm outside!" Hank declared, throwing his hands in the air toward the sunset.

I'd just met Hank a few hours earlier. We'd spent an unusually warm October afternoon slinging lures for bass from the deck of a boat owned by our mutual friend Darrin. It'd been a picturesque fall day. The leaves on the cottonwoods lining the lake shimmered like polished gold bullion, and geese by the thousands had flown over our heads as they trekked south for warmer waters. Winter was coming. This would likely be our last fishing trip of the year.

Hank caught his best fish that day on a Berkley prop bait. My best had slammed a Strike King Popping Perch. Darrin, in typical fashion, while managing the trolling motor to put his friends in the best spots, had outfished Hank and me that evening. His largest was a thick-bellied twenty-inch largemouth. It had exploded from the bulrushes to slam his spinnerbait like an NFL linebacker.

At the end of the evening, the three of us stood on Darrin's dock and marveled at the sunset. Not even Monet could have captured the wonders of the sky that evening. Sunsets in the Midwest during harvest are explosions of red, orange, gold, and yellow. Walt Whitman described them as "pure luminous color fighting the silent shadows to the last."[34]

As we feasted our eyes on the ever-changing art, Hank raised his hands and declared his nearness to God.

Any angler reading this can agree with Hank's sentiment. Something about being outside, especially near water, makes us feel close to God. But what is that something, and why is this such a universal experience?

The apostle Paul gives us the answer in Romans when he writes, "[God's] invisible attributes, namely, his eternal power and divine nature, have been clearly perceived, ever since the creation of the world, in the things that have been made" (1:20a).

In this passage, Paul describes how both the godless and the God-fearing see God in creation. This is the doctrine of *general revelation*. God reveals Himself through His creation in a way that even the one who denies His existence can't help but see. Whether you're a Christian or not, to behold a snowcapped mountain or gaze across an ocean is to see the eternal power and divine nature of your Maker.

This is why rugged places summon effusive statements of thanksgiving to God more than, say, parking lots, amusement parks, or shopping malls. Undeveloped, wild places fix our eyes *directly on* God's power and nature. God is God no matter where we are.

It's true that the One who created freestone rivers and crater lakes is just as present with us when we're stuck in rush-hour traffic or waiting in a checkout line at the store. He is just as glorious when we're looking at a computer screen as when we're staring at a sunset. Yet not all places light us up inside in the same way. When was the last time you got out of your vehicle in bumper-to-bumper traffic, threw your hands into the air, and declared, "I feel so close to God when I'm surrounded by concrete structures"?

I'm guessing it's never happened.

But I'm also guessing you've had moments atop a mountain or in a trout stream when *Thank You, God!* flowed from your heart and out your mouth. Wild, rugged places allow us to gaze upon God without anything artificial or man-made blocking our vision.

This is why wild, rugged places humble us. Standing before a Nebraska sunset, a Colorado mountain, or one of Canada's expansive lakes reminds our souls that we are infinitely tiny compared to the One who designed these wonders. They instruct us on the truth that our Creator needs nothing. He's infinitely sufficient. Infinitely powerful. Infinitely satisfied. He didn't need to create water to be refreshed. He didn't need to make fish or galaxies to feel productive. And He didn't need to make you and me in order to have companionship.

In this way, these outdoor wonders are a constant reminder that everything God has made is a gift and must be received as such. As Ken Myers, one of my favorite teachers, said, "The ordering presence of love in all things requires the recognition that creation is a gift, and that the proper posture of the creatures is always one of gratitude."[35]

There are few formulas in life, but this is one I've found: go to a vast wilderness or stand beside a raging sea, and you will feel thankful.

Guaranteed. If you stand on a dock with two friends and gaze into a Midwest sunset, you will throw your hands in the air and declare your nearness to God. It just happens.

QUESTIONS FOR FURTHER REFLECTION:

1. Which places outdoors do you visit to see God fill your cup with awe and wonder? How do you see the power and nature of God in those wild, rugged spaces?
2. What place has been the least inspiring or awe-evoking for you?
3. God didn't need to make anything, which means everything in our lives is a gift. How does recognizing the givenness of all things—understanding that all things in life are a gift from God—enable you to give thanks to God for every person, place, and event in your life?

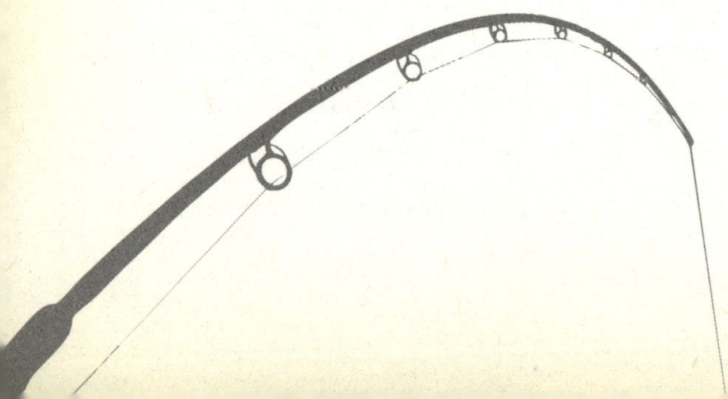

40

FISH TO BE AMAZED

We tell ourselves we're cursed or chosen, blasphemed or blessed. It's simply too hard to accept that a huge part of the equation doesn't depend on us.

David Coggins, *The Optimist*

Scripture to Read: Ecclesiastes 7:1–14; 1 Corinthians 13:1–13

I first approached fly fishing wearing the lab coat of a researcher. For the first two years after college, I worked as a graduate assistant for the University of Nebraska. I partnered with Nebraska Game and Parks to conduct studies on the rearing density of trout during their fry (the period when they are six to eight weeks old) and parr (from eight weeks to release) stages of life. I recorded the weights, lengths, and hematocrit readings for hundreds of trout during the day. In the late afternoon, I'd clean up my work area and drive twelve miles up the road to fly fish on Gracie Creek.

When I say I approached fly fishing wearing the lab coat of a researcher, I don't mean that I wore the actual jacket to the river. I didn't. I hung it on a hook by the front door of the Calamus Fish Hatchery before heading out to fish. But jacket or no jacket, I carried the same cold, calculated mindset toward fly fishing that I applied to my research project. I tried to figure everything out, crack every code, and solve every problem. I felt that if I hoped to succeed, I had to master all the variables. Those days, I carried two scientific journals in the passenger seat of my Volkswagen Beetle: one for my research at the hatchery and one for my studies at Gracie Creek.

I caught a lot of fish but didn't have much fun. I wasn't driving to the water to experience the simple pleasures that fishing offers. I went to learn all there was to know so I could feel like an expert. Ambitions in my head crowded out the chance of being thrilled in my heart.

One day, I shared these thoughts with Ron, a biologist at the Calamus Hatchery who was also an elder in our local church. Ron suggested I read the book of Ecclesiastes. I did, and it impacted me so profoundly that I've read it a couple of times a year every year since.

Ecclesiastes begins, "The words of the Preacher, the son of David, king in Jerusalem. Vanity of vanities, says the Preacher, vanity of vanities! All is vanity" (1:1–2).

When I first read those words, I thought Solomon was saying that life lacked purpose and meaning. I tend to look for purpose in everything—I'm a meaning-seeking beast—so those first two sentences bothered me. But as I continued to read, I realized Solomon wasn't declaring the purposelessness of life. He was describing the meaninglessness of trying to figure everything out.

Behind the English word *vanity* in the passage is the Hebrew word *hevel*. It means "breath" or "vapor." The preacher is saying that everything in life is elusive and beyond us. It's impossible to perfectly understand any given subject because, by the time you lean in to study it, like a vapor—*poof*—it's gone. For us to aim at solving all of life's riddles would be a futile, vain ambition.

Solomon knew this better than anyone. Remember, this is the man whom God had given "wisdom and understanding beyond measure, and breadth of mind like the sand on the seashore, so that Solomon's wisdom surpassed the wisdom of all the people of the east and all the wisdom of Egypt" (1 Kings 4:29b–30).

Solomon reached the pinnacle of knowledge and success relative to all other human beings at the time. If he had found peace and pleasure forevermore in those accomplishments, he wouldn't have written, "All is vanity!" Especially not in his opening lines! If making superior knowledge the aim of his life had imbued his heart with meaning, he wouldn't have written, "Vanity of vanities!"

Solomon wasn't declaring the purposelessness of life. He was describing the meaninglessness of trying to figure everything out.

Solomon said, "[God] has put eternity into man's heart." This has a poetic ring to it, but Solomon was explaining why we live with an ever-present angst. Here's the entire statement: "[God] has put eternity into man's heart, yet *so that he cannot find out what God has done from the beginning to the end*" (Eccl. 3:11b).

Eternity in our hearts drives us to try to understand the beginning, middle, and end of all matters. We are purpose-driven, meaning-seeking, want-to-have-it-all creatures. We want to know what God knows. But we can't. That's Solomon's point. The sooner we come to terms with our finite, limited capacity to know what God knows, the sooner we'll enjoy what God gives us to enjoy.

Solomon was not a wet blanket. He had a deep love for God and God's people. One of my favorite teachers was Haddon Robinson. He said in class once, "Solomon is not a cynic or a skeptic. He's a realist and a person of faith ... deep faith, which shows itself throughout the entire book."

Solomon also wrote most of the book of Proverbs. From Proverbs we learn that Solomon longed to help God's people experience *shalom*: life-giving peace with God, one another, and all creation. He wrote Ecclesiastes with the same aim, presenting three main ideas to give us a vision. Each of the three sections is vital for understanding the entire work.

The first movement is the one we've already discussed. Solomon opened with statements about life's futility, meaninglessness, and vanity.

I'll mention the final movement before mentioning the middle section. At the end of the book, Solomon summed up the entire message. This truth is not only a conclusion to the book but also the proper aim of our lives. Here are the last two verses of Ecclesiastes:

> The end of the matter; all has been heard. Fear God and keep his commandments, for this is the whole duty of man. For God will bring every deed into judgment, with every secret thing, whether good or evil. (12:13–14)

Solomon opened his magnum opus with "Life is impossible to figure out," and he closed it with "So, fear God and keep His commandments." We can't see all things perfectly, but God can and does. He perceives all, knows all, and will perfectly judge all in the end. These are the first and last sections, the bookends on either side of the middle.

The message of the middle? Keep life simple. Stay humble. Enjoy what God puts before us without vainly trying to figure it all out. Consider this sampling of verses from the middle section of the book:

- I saw that there is nothing better than that a man should rejoice in his work, for that is his lot. Who can bring him to see what will be after him? (3:22)
- In the day of prosperity be joyful, and in the day of adversity consider: God has made the one as well as the other, so that man may not find out anything that will be after him. (7:14)
- I commend joy, for man has nothing better under the sun but to eat and drink and be joyful, for this will go with him in his toil through the days of his life that God has given him under the sun. (8:15)
- Go, eat your bread with joy, and drink your wine with a merry heart, for God has already approved what you do. (9:7)

Life is jam-packed with meaning and purpose. Solomon knew this better than we do. But he also knew that if our greatest aim is to figure it all out so we can feel like experts, we'll waste our lives and miss the everyday gifts God gives us: graces such as work, family, friendship, food, and drink.

And fishing.

Upon reading Ecclesiastes, I threw away my Gracie Creek research journal.

(For a season. I'll always be a student at heart.)

As I mentioned earlier in the devotion on syncing up to God's rhythms (chapter 34), I believe our pleasure in fishing is enhanced as we figure things out. My problem in those early years was that figuring things out was the primary reason I fished. I fished to feel pride. I fished to prove myself.

My goal is different now. Today, I fish to be amazed by God. I go to the water to be humbled. And I always arrive with open arms (and a landing net), ready to receive whatever slimy, gorgeously spotted gifts God might dazzle me with that day.

May you be dazzled and delighted by the Lord during your times on the water as well!

QUESTIONS FOR FURTHER REFLECTION:

1. Are there areas in life that you are overthinking or trying to master in order to feel or sound like an expert? How could surrendering those areas to the majesty and wisdom of God help you experience joy?
2. What are the simple gifts of God in your life that He wants you to enjoy every day?
3. What does it look like to fear God and obey His commands while enjoying your relationships, work, and the other simple pleasures in life?

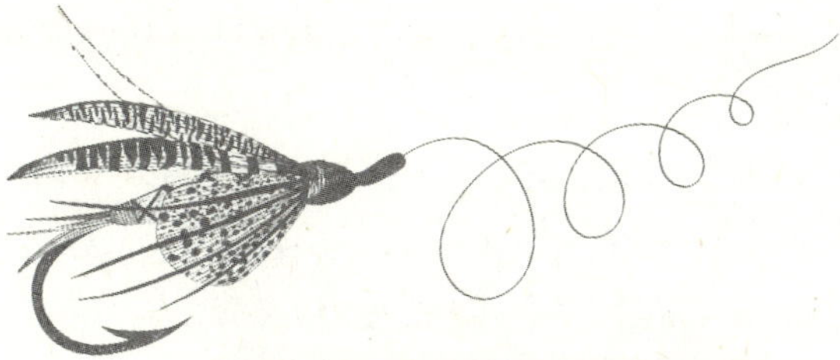

AFTERWORD

Jay Yelas

Oh, the depth of the riches of the wisdom and
knowledge of God!
How unsearchable his judgments,
and his paths beyond tracing out!
"Who has known the mind of the Lord?
Or who has been his counselor?"
"Who has ever given to God,
that God should repay them?"
For from him and through him and for him are all
things.
To him be the glory forever! Amen.
(Rom. 11:33–36 NIV)

God is so great, my fellow anglers. I'm so thankful we can experience and enjoy Him together through fishing.

I've had the pleasure of fishing as a born-again, Spirit-filled lover of Jesus for over thirty years. The journey has been a delight because it has brought me closer to our heavenly Father. The Lord has taught me so much through fishing, giving me solid life lessons while drawing me nearer to Him.

Now that you have finished *The Far Bank*, I hope you will continue the journey of profoundly knowing and enjoying our Father in heaven. It begins, continues, and never moves past studying and obeying the Word of God. Solomon writes in Proverbs 1:7: "The fear of the LORD is the beginning of knowledge, but fools despise wisdom and instruction" (NIV).

As a young man, I dreamed of becoming a pro bass fisherman. I worked at it hard in my own strength, without faith in God, with limited results for the first two years of my career. That's when I met Jesus. On February 28, 1993, my life and work took on an entirely new trajectory after I heard the gospel and received Jesus Christ as my Lord and Savior. I started fearing the Lord and seeking His wisdom.

The fear of the Lord is an appreciation for who God is: He is our creator and the sustainer of life. He gives us new life through the work of His Son, Jesus, who died as payment for our sins. The fear of the Lord doesn't mean we're afraid of God; it means we revere Him and remain in awe of His power and glory. It's to live in the knowledge of His great love for us expressed through His Son, Jesus. My fear of the Lord made me want to submit to Him my life and career as a professional fisherman.

I'm inexpressibly grateful to God for my success on the water. Philippians 2:13 says, "It is God who works in you to will and to act in order to fulfill his good purpose" (NIV). Apparently, it must have been His good purpose and will to see my career as a bass pro take off, because it did.

I worked hard, but God alone determines outcomes. He's been so good to me, blessing me every step of the way. Therefore, I've always tried to give Him all the glory in my mind and heart. I enjoyed a thirty-five-year Hall of Fame career, winning several titles and even an ESPY Award. None of this would have occurred if I hadn't surrendered my fishing career to Jesus. I'm sure of this fact.

This leads to one of my encouragements for you, fellow angler: remain humble. This is one of the most important lessons I've learned throughout my career. James writes, "But he gives us more grace. That is why Scripture says: 'God opposes the proud but shows favor to the humble'" (4:6 NIV).

God highly values humility. Jesus displayed it better than any human being who ever lived. Born in a manger, a servant His entire life, He is our clearest example. Humility is crucial in your relationship with God, but it also makes you a better angler. In that sense, I'm offering you a fishing tip: Humility. Adaptability. Teachableness. Great fishermen learn to read the current conditions and adjust their techniques according to water levels, weather changes, and fishing pressure. They don't pridefully force their ideas on the fish; instead, they humbly "listen to the fish" as the best way to catch them that day.

I am now retired from the Bassmaster Elite Series and have more time to enjoy the many other ways to experience and enjoy God through fishing. My passion has shifted a bit; I now focus on taking other people fishing and helping them have a memorable day on the water. These days, I spend much of my time leading the C.A.S.T. for Kids Foundation. Our mission is to enrich the lives of children with special needs, support their families, and strengthen communities through the sport of fishing. We are a volunteer-based nonprofit that organizes fishing events across America to celebrate special kids.

God has really blessed the C.A.S.T. for Kids Foundation. His heart has always been to serve and care for "the least of these" (see Matt. 25:40). Amazing things happen at C.A.S.T. for Kids events when people from diverse parts of a community come together to celebrate the less fortunate in their community. Fishing is a great equalizer, and it brings people together. It's also a great training ground for discipleship. I'm trying to follow Jesus' example as the One who didn't come to be served but to serve.

Fishing has been a thread of God's goodness that He's weaved throughout my life. Fishing has been my occupation, my ministry, and a way to serve others, blessing children with special needs and whole communities. My favorite memories of fishing include times with my wife and daughters. Getting together with old friends annually for a fishing trip and renewing our friendships is always life-giving. Quality time on the water with those we love is a light in a dark world.

God is so big and vast that I can't tell you how He does it all, but I can tell you that all His promises are true. He loves His children and only ever does what is good for them, as Romans 8:28 says, "We know that in all things God works for the good of those who love him, who have been called according to his purpose" (NIV).

You've finished *The Far Bank*. Way to go! I hope you will continue to develop an intimate relationship with God through His

Son, Jesus, as you study the Scriptures. Make reading the Bible and praying to God as your Father a part of your daily routine.

Then, be on the lookout for God on your next fishing trip. He will be there!

Jay Yelas
C.A.S.T. for Kids Foundation—Executive Director
2002 Bassmaster Classic Champion
2020 Inductee to the Bass Fishing Hall of Fame

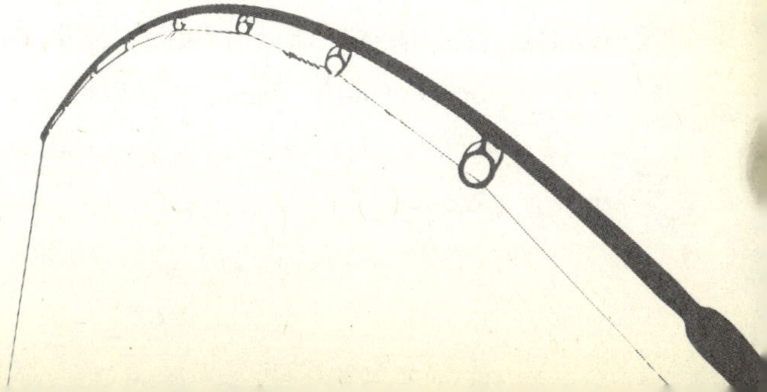

ACKNOWLEDGMENTS

Several friends and family members played integral roles throughout this writing project: Don Pape, my agent extraordinaire; Luke McKinnon, my editor and fellow fly fisherman; Jeff Gerke, my content editor, who helped clarify and improve the ideas in this book; Mary Pipher, my mother and loyal reader; and Jay Yelas, who not only wrote the afterword but also allowed me to tell one of his stories in this book. I'm also grateful to Heartland's staff and elders for supporting me throughout this project.

I'd be remiss if I didn't mention my fishing buddies, my friends who have tirelessly and with great sacrifice helped me research the subject of this book. These men put on their waders or fired up their boats to help create many of the stories in *The Far Bank*: Mark McHargue, Adrian Smith, Darrin Brumbaugh, Matt Green, Bryan Nokelby, Travis Purkerson, Dillon Purkerson, Nathan Musgrave, Scott Ratliff, Les Griess, Bob Seeger, Larry Myers, Steve Beyers, Armando Diaz, Butch Chojnacki, Dan Carroll, Thom Ludtke, Dave Ludtke, Christian Ludtke, Bryan Clark, Aidan Pipher, and Elijah Green. I'm eager to continue our research in the years ahead!

I'd like to express my deepest gratitude to my family for supporting my work and play, writing and fishing. Jamie, my true companion and favorite person to impress; Kate, Aidan and his wife Ellie, and Claire, my children, who deserve a hero's share of rewards in heaven for being the subjects of an incalculable number of sermon and book illustrations; Jim and Mary Pipher, my parents, who planned our family vacations to include incredible meals and breathtaking scenery, in that order; and RB and Bev Drickey, my in-laws, who took me to their secret fishing ponds even before I married their daughter. (Bev, thanks again for holding the pole as I caught *my* Master Angler bass.)

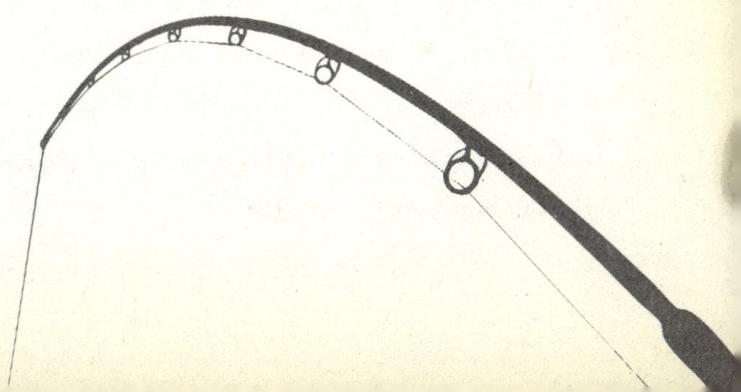

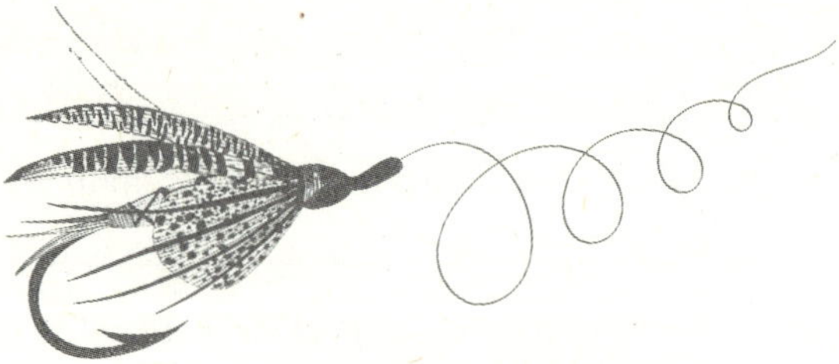

APPENDIX

Intentional Discussions with The Far Bank

I wrote *The Far Bank* with the hope that it would help families, friends, and fishing buddies have intentional conversations. In our busy lives, it's easy to overlook the importance of making space for authentic spiritual discussions with those on the journey with us. Toward that end, here are seven suggestions for how you might use *The Far Bank* together:

1. On a fishing trip: Something about being outside near water inspires conversation among friends. Add a firepit to the mix, and you have a recipe for honest, encouraging discussions. Here's an idea for how to use this book as a guide and conversation starter on your next fishing trip with friends or family:

Step 1: Have each person read the same devotion in the morning during their time alone with the Lord. You could also read it aloud together during breakfast (without answering the questions).

Step 2: Enjoy the day and catch a lot of fish.

Step 3: At the end of the day, during the evening meal or while warming your toes by a campfire, have everyone reflect on the morning's devotion. What did the Scripture and devotion inspire you to think about while fishing?

Step 4: Have each person answer the questions listed at the end of that devotion.

Step 5: Repeat steps 1–4 each day of the trip. If you're taking a five-day trip, here are five chapters for your consideration:

- Chapter 3—Mystery and Paradox
- Chapter 12—Water
- Chapter 16—Anglers, Really?
- Chapter 27—The Good, Imperfect Gift
- Chapter 34—Rhythms

2. In a weekly small group: There are forty devotions in *The Far Bank*, a perfect number for a small group to go through in a year, perhaps taking a few weeks off in the summer and during holidays. There's something powerful that takes place when friends meet regularly. Conversations go below the surface, trust deepens, and the bonds of friendship strengthen. When you meet to read and discuss a chapter of *The Far Bank*, answer the questions and pray for one another's relationship with Jesus. In addition, consider creating a goal or challenge for the week that each member will report on the following week.

3. In an online group discussion: Consider creating a Facebook group or interactive blog that you and your angling friends could use to walk through these forty devotions. You can post prayer requests, additional passages of Scripture, and even photos of your successes on the water. An online group discussion can be a tremendous encouragement when you can't meet in person.

4. As a summer reading project for high school and college-aged students: If you're a pastor, youth leader, or mentor, consider challenging the young men and women in your life to work through *The Far Bank* during their summer break. Consider meeting once a week to have a group conversation about some of their reflections and answers to the questions in each chapter.

5. In family devotional time: Daily devotions are a foundation-building experience for families. When a mother or father pulls the family together to read and discuss the truths of God, they help strengthen their children's faith in Christ. Consider reading *The Far Bank* as a family, reading a devotion each day or perhaps one a week.

6. As a gift for a friend: Darrin is one of my close friends and fishing partners—I mentioned him in chapter 39, "It's All a Gift." He's also a business owner who wants to encourage his clients spiritually as well as serve them through his work. Darrin gives *The Far Bank* to the people he serves to celebrate his love for fishing and his even greater passion for Jesus. Consider giving *The Far Bank* to a friend and inviting them to read through it on the same schedule and meet regularly to discuss your thoughts.

7. As an on-the-water gift: Most anglers I know are generous. They'll give flies or lures to people they meet on the water. They'll give their time to teach others how to fish. They'll even occasionally share their favorite spots and hard-earned fishing tips with strangers. I wrote *The Far Bank* hoping it would be another way for you to practice your generosity. Let me challenge you to keep a couple of copies of *The Far Bank* in your vehicle or tackle box to give away to the new friends you meet on the water. You'll be sharing your love for fishing and your even deeper passion for Christ with those you meet while fishing your favorite waters.

ENDNOTES

1. Kenneth Grahame, *The Wind in the Willows* (New York: Barnes and Noble, 1995), 6.

2. Herman Bavinck, *The Wonderful Works of God: Instruction in the Christian Religion according to the Reformed Confession* (Glenside, PA: Westminster Seminary Press, 2019), 12.

3. Bavinck, *The Wonderful Works of God*, 18.

4. C. S. Lewis, *George MacDonald: An Anthology* (New York: HarperCollins, 1973), xxiii, emphasis added.

5. Michael Reeves, *Delighting in the Trinity: An Introduction to the Christian Faith* (Downers Grove, IL: InterVarsity, 2012), 76.

6. Augustine, *The Works of Augustine: A Translation for the 21st Century* (New York: New City Press, 1990), 41.

7. John Calvin, *The Institutes of the Christian Religion*, trans. Henry Beveridge (Grand Rapids, MI: Wm. B. Eerdmans, 2001), Book 1, chap. 1, https://oll.libertyfund.org/titles/calvin-the-institutes-of-the-christian-religion.

8. David James Duncan, *The River Why* (San Francisco: Sierra Club Books, 1983), 8.

9. Thomas Brooks, *Precious Remedies against Satan's Devices: A Companion for Christians of All Denominations* (Philadelphia: Jonathan Pounder, 1810), 16.

10. David Foster Wallace, *This Is Water: Some Thoughts, Delivered on a Significant Occasion, about Living a Compassionate Life* (New York: Little, Brown, 2009), 35–39.

11. Elizabeth Rembert, "Drought Has Dried Up Rivers and Lakes, Revealing Abandoned Towns and Shipwrecks," KCUR, August 25, 2022, www.kcur.org/news/2022-08-25/drought-and-history#.

12. Bavinck, *The Wonderful Works of God*, 299.

13. D. Martyn Lloyd-Jones, *Spiritual Depression: Its Causes and Cure* (Grand Rapids, MI: Wm. B. Eerdmans, 1965), 21.

14. Ben Westcott, "Is This the World's Largest Pearl? It's Been under a Bed for 10 Years," CNN, August 25, 2016, www.cnn.com/style/article/largest-pearl-philippines-amurao/index.html.

15. Bavinck, *The Wonderful Works of God*, 378–79.

16. Reeves, *Delighting in the Trinity*, 91.

17. Michael Ruhlman, *Ruhlman's Twenty: 20 Techniques, 100 Recipes, A Cook's Manifesto* (San Francisco: Chronicle Books, 2011), 18.

18. Rudolf Schnackenburg, *The Gospel of Matthew* (Grand Rapids, MI: Wm. B. Eerdmans, 2002), 51.

19. Keith Sutton, "58 Years of Arkansas Fishing Records," *Arkansas Democrat Gazette*, March 26, 2017, www.arkansasonline.com/news/2017/mar/26/58-years-arkansas-fishing-records/.

20. Keith Sutton, "These Strange-but-True Fishing Tales Will Amaze You," *Arkansas Democrat Gazette*, April 8, 2018, www.arkansasonline.com/news/2018/apr/08/these-strange-true-fishing-tales-will-amaze-you/.

21. Michel de Montaigne, *Essays of Michel de Montaigne*, ed. William Carew Hazlitt, trans. Charles Cotton, Book 3, chap. 11, https://www.gutenberg.org/files/3600/3600-h/3600-h.htm#link2HCH0104.

22. Gavin Ortlund, *Humility: The Joy of Self-Forgetfulness* (Wheaton, IL: Crossway, 2023), xvi.

23. "Turn Your Eyes Upon Jesus," Helen H. Lemmel, *Worship and Service Hymnal for Church, School, and Home* (Chicago: Hope, 1957), 220.

24. Bavinck, *The Wonderful Works of God*, 170.

25. Sebastian Junger, *Tribe: On Homecoming and Belonging* (New York: Hachette, 2016), xvii.

26. The Gospel Coalition, "Friendship and Gospel Culture," *YouTube*, May 26, 2022, www.youtube.com/watch?v=v5UaEaDLXOYandt=589s.

27. Dietrich Bonhoeffer, *Life Together: The Classic Exploration of Christian Community* (New York: HarperCollins, 1954), 27–28.

28. Kirk Wallace Johnson, *The Feather Thief: Beauty, Obsession, and the Natural History Heist of the Century* (New York: Penguin, 2018), 63.

29. Kevin Vanhoozer, *The Drama of Doctrine: A Canonical-Linguistic Approach to Christian Theology* (Louisville, KY: Westminster John Knox Press, 2005), 16.

30. Don Carson, "A Miracle Full of Surprises (Part 3): John 11:1–53," The Gospel Coalition, December 6, 2008, www.thegospelcoalition.org/sermon/a-miracle-full-of-surprises-john-11-part-3-of-5/.

31. Bavinck, *The Wonderful Works of God*, 465.

32. George Herbert, *The Works of George Herbert*, vol. 1 (London: Pickering, 1836), 168.

33. Cormac McCarthy, *The Road* (New York: Vintage Books, 2006), 286–87.

34. Walt Whitman, "A Prairie Sunset," The Walt Whitman Archive, accessed November 21, 2024, https://whitmanarchive.org/item/per.00119.

35. Mars Hill Audio, Mars Hill Audio Journal, Volume 112, March 7, 2014, https://mha-members.org/journals/mars-hill-audio-journal-volume-112.